A CHRISTMAS

COLORING BOOK

by Christea Blue

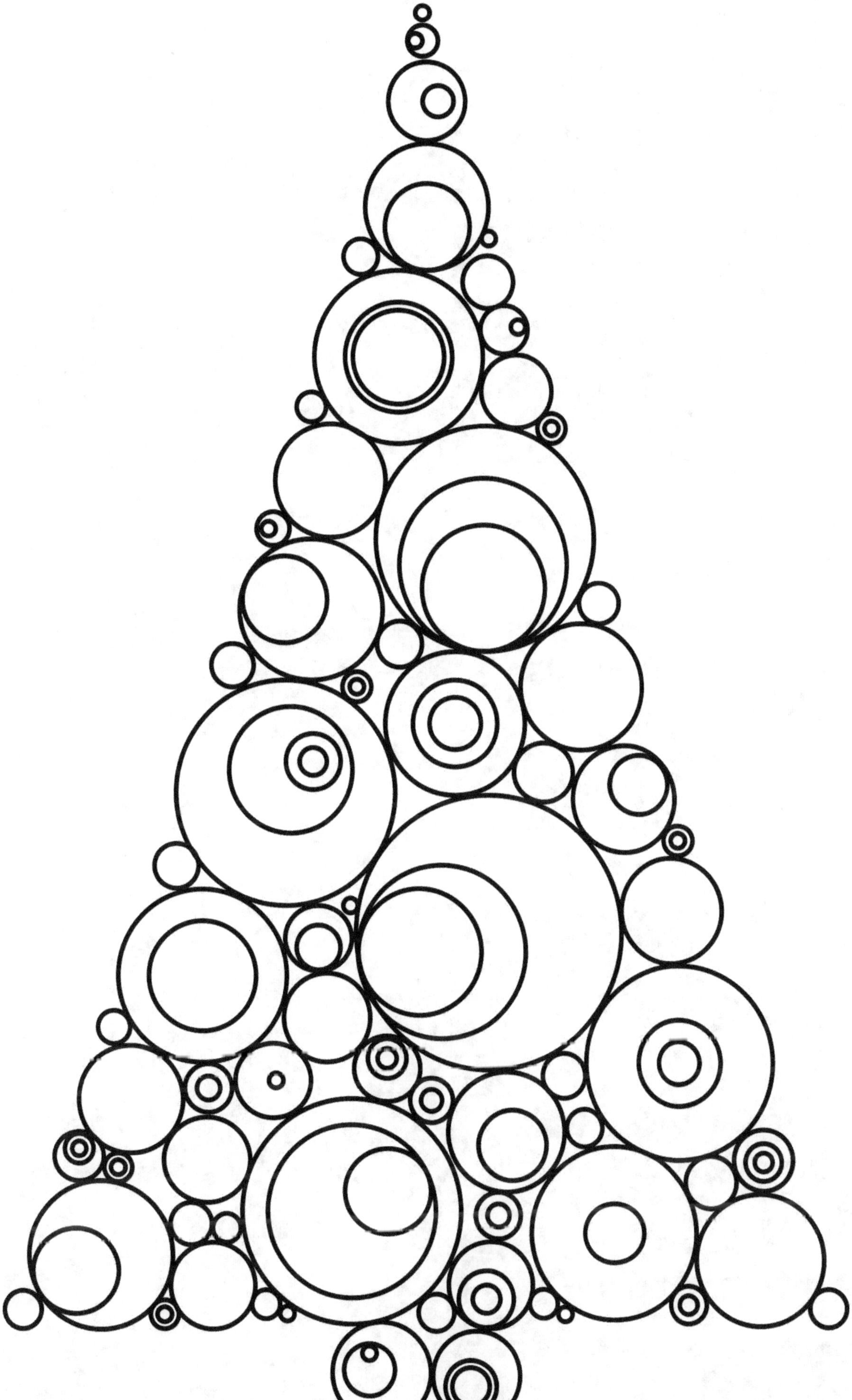

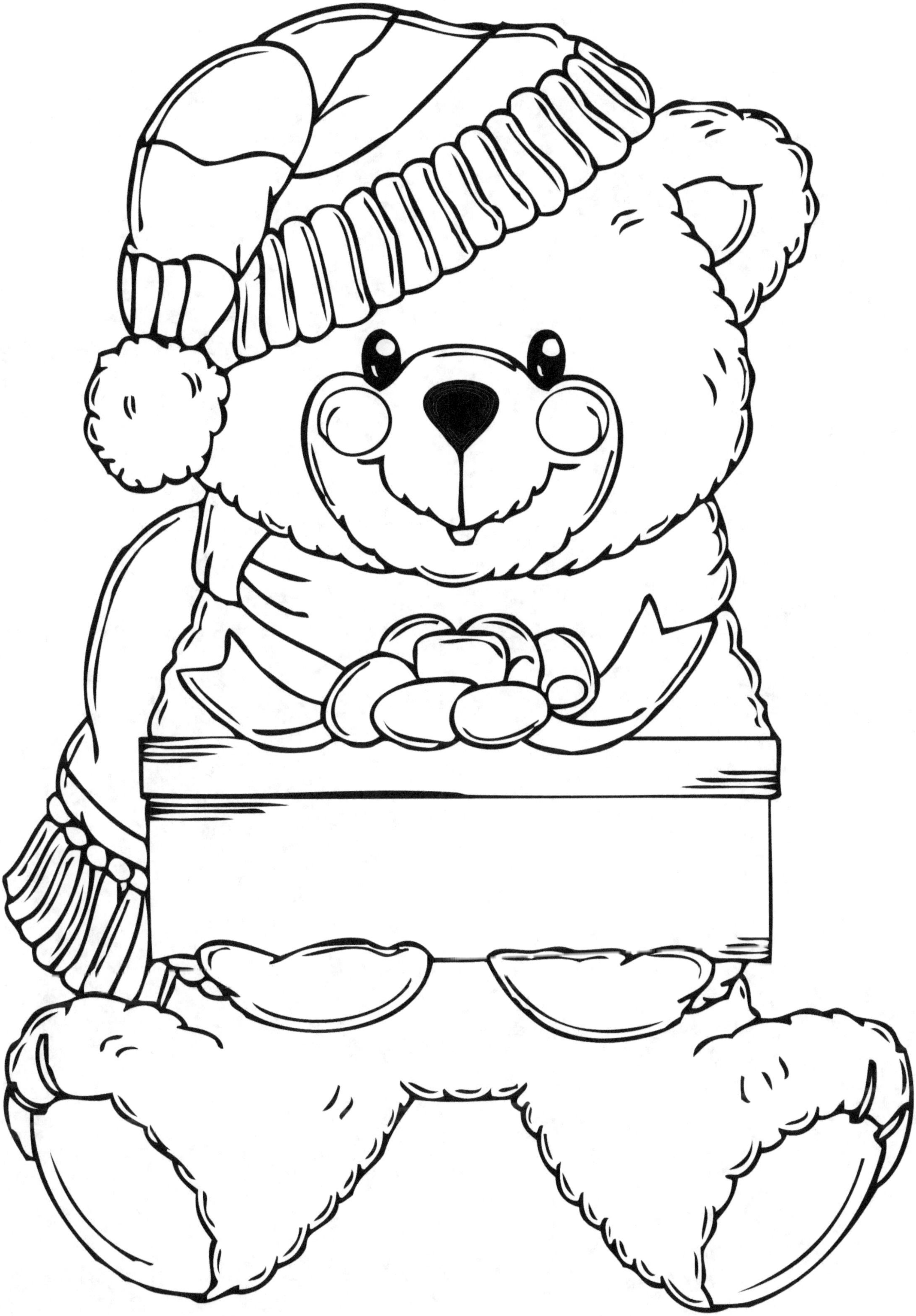

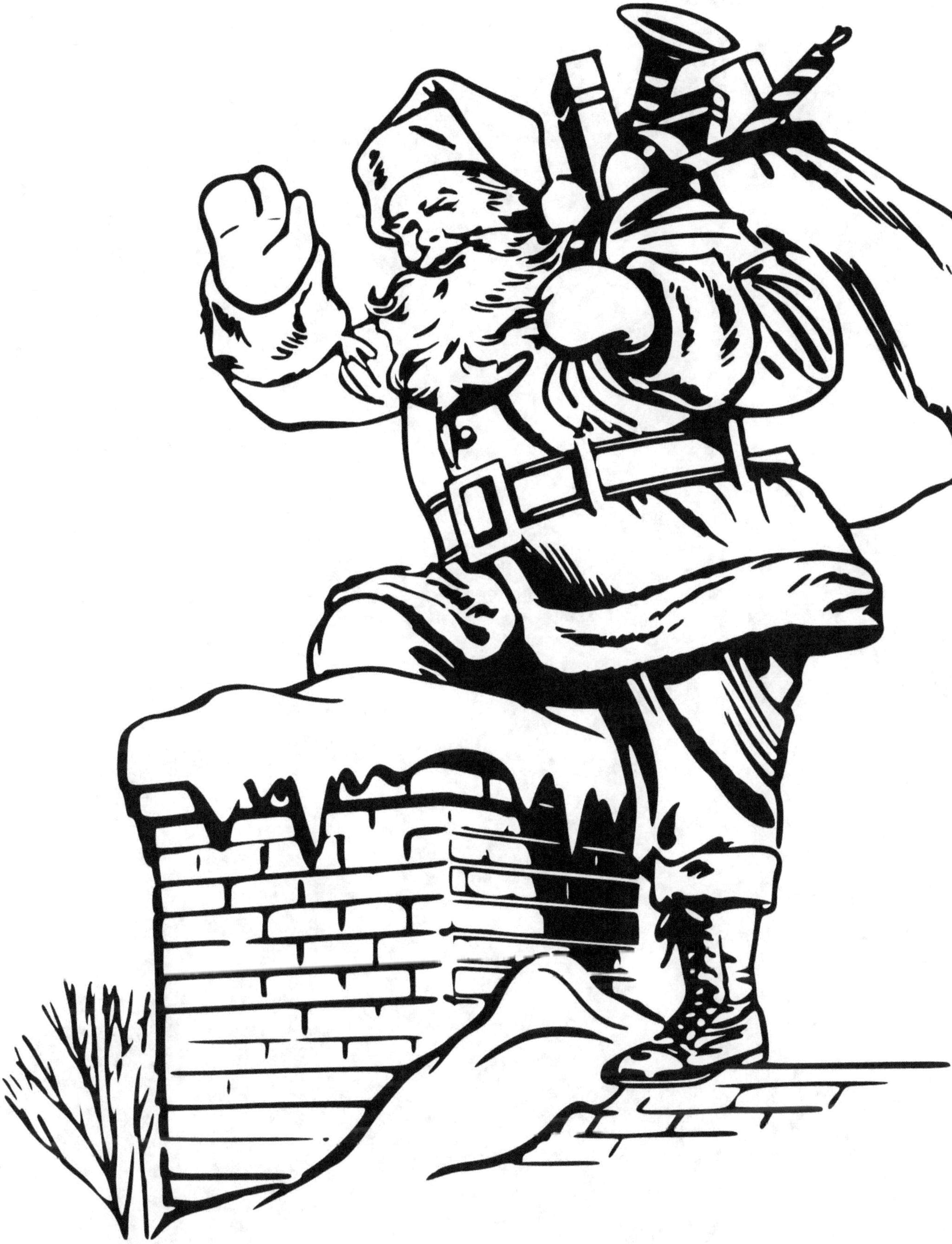

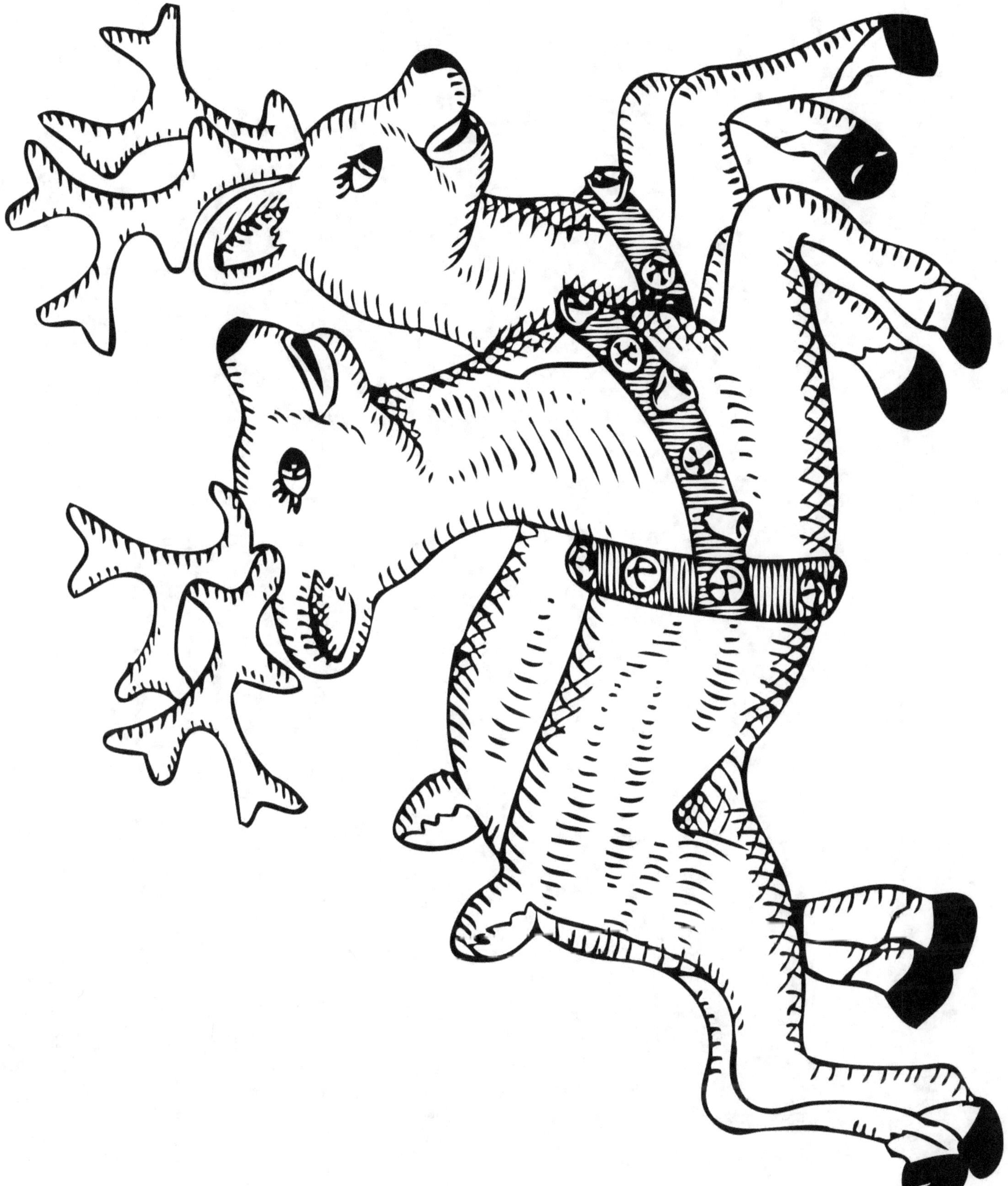

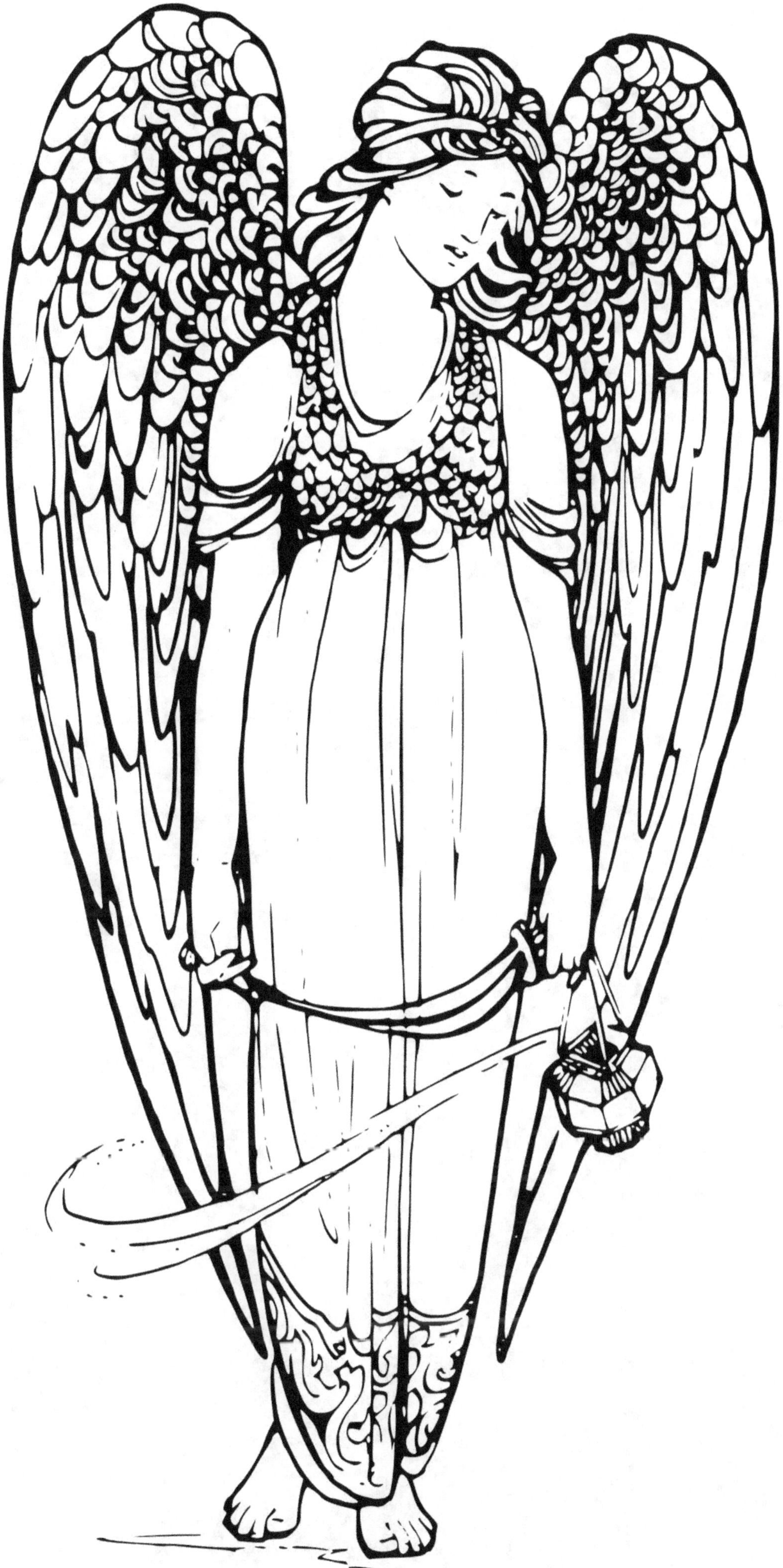

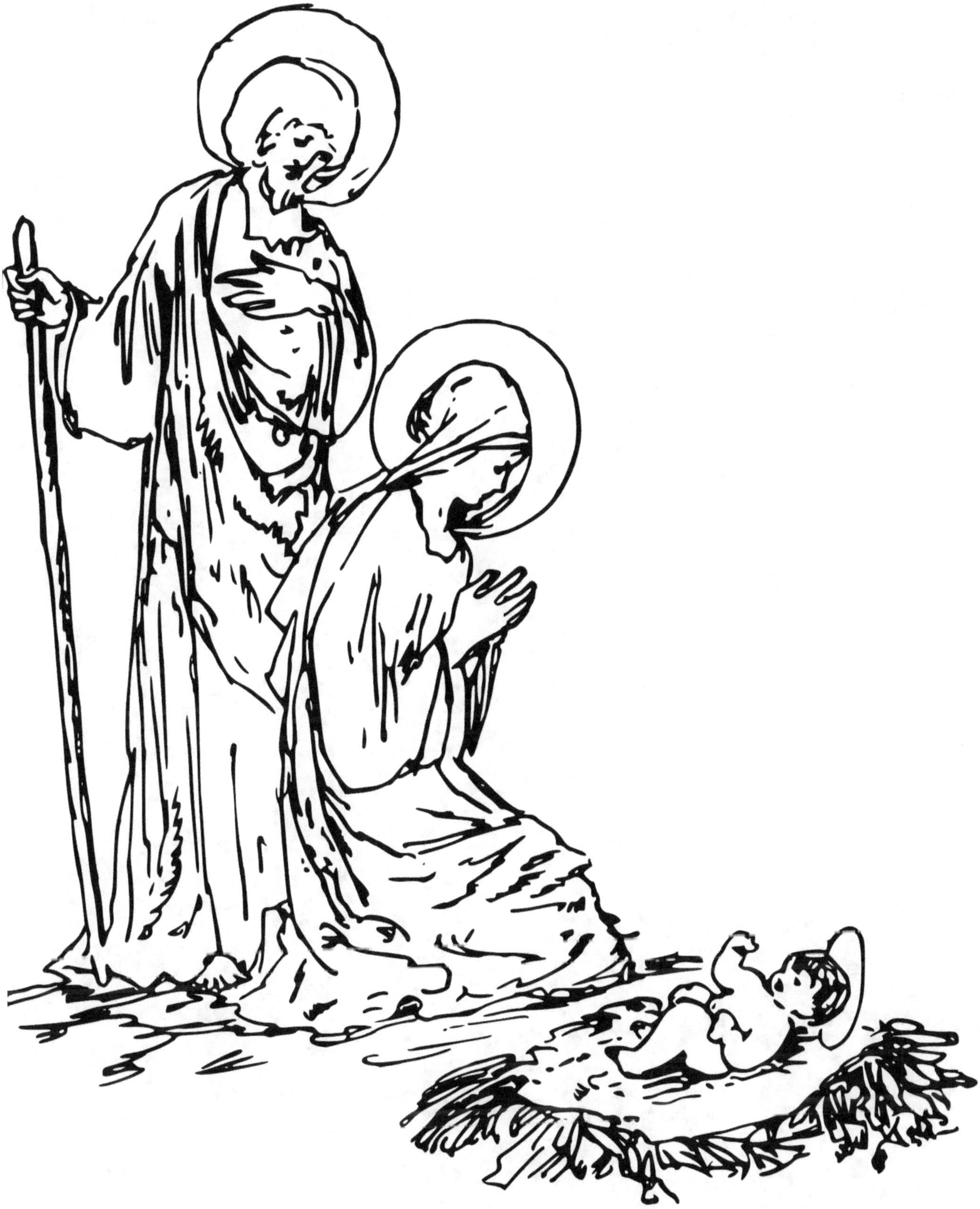

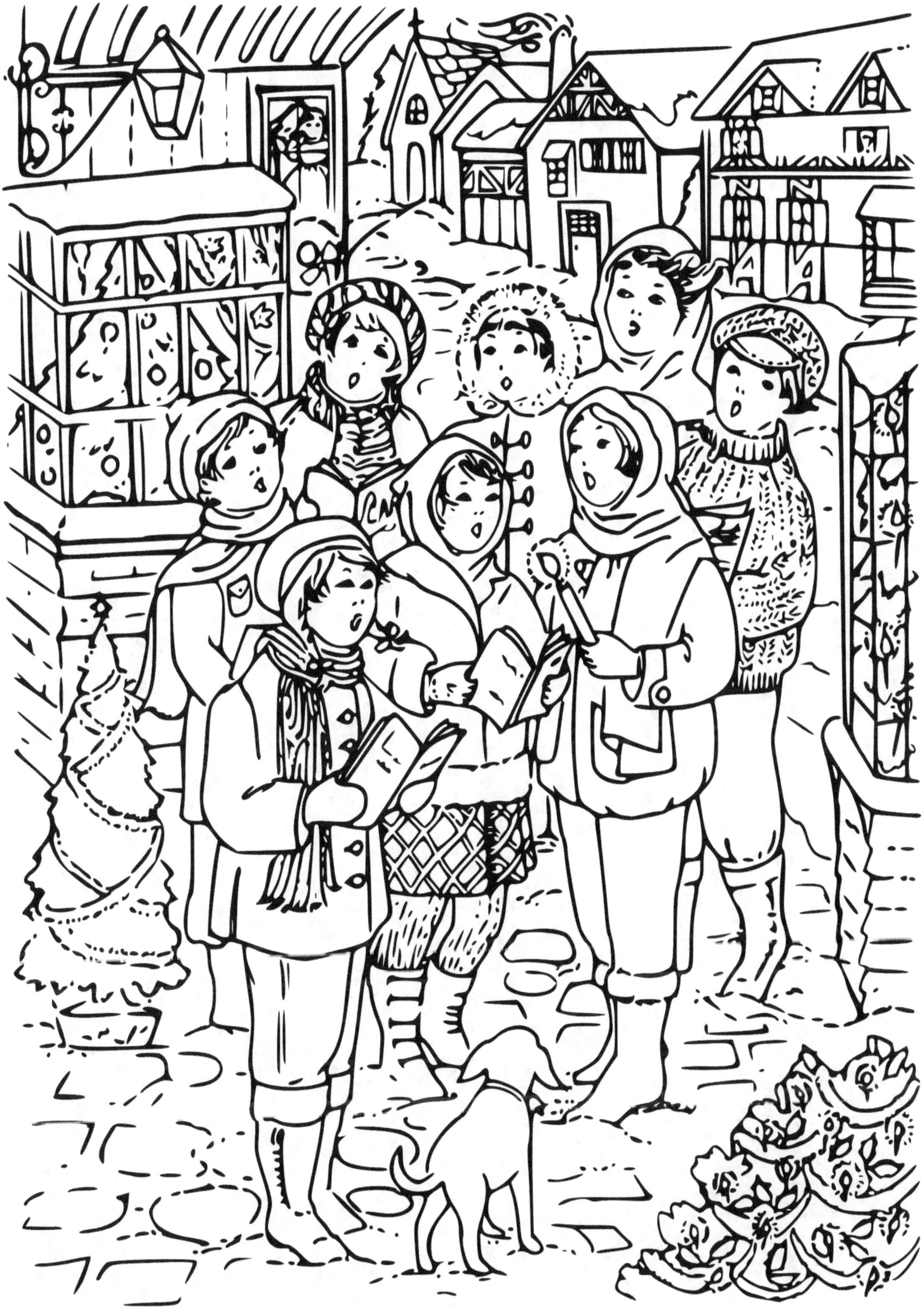

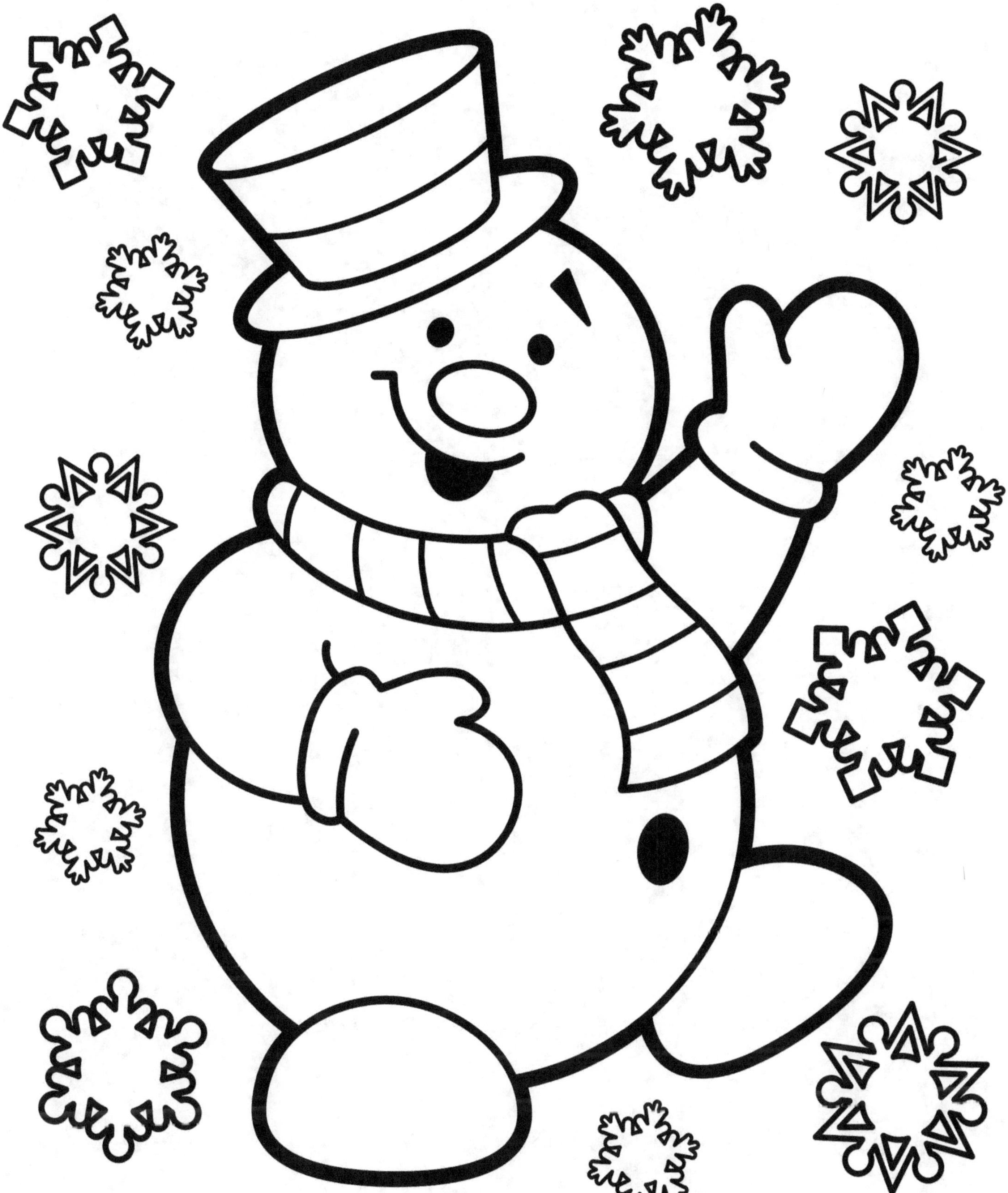

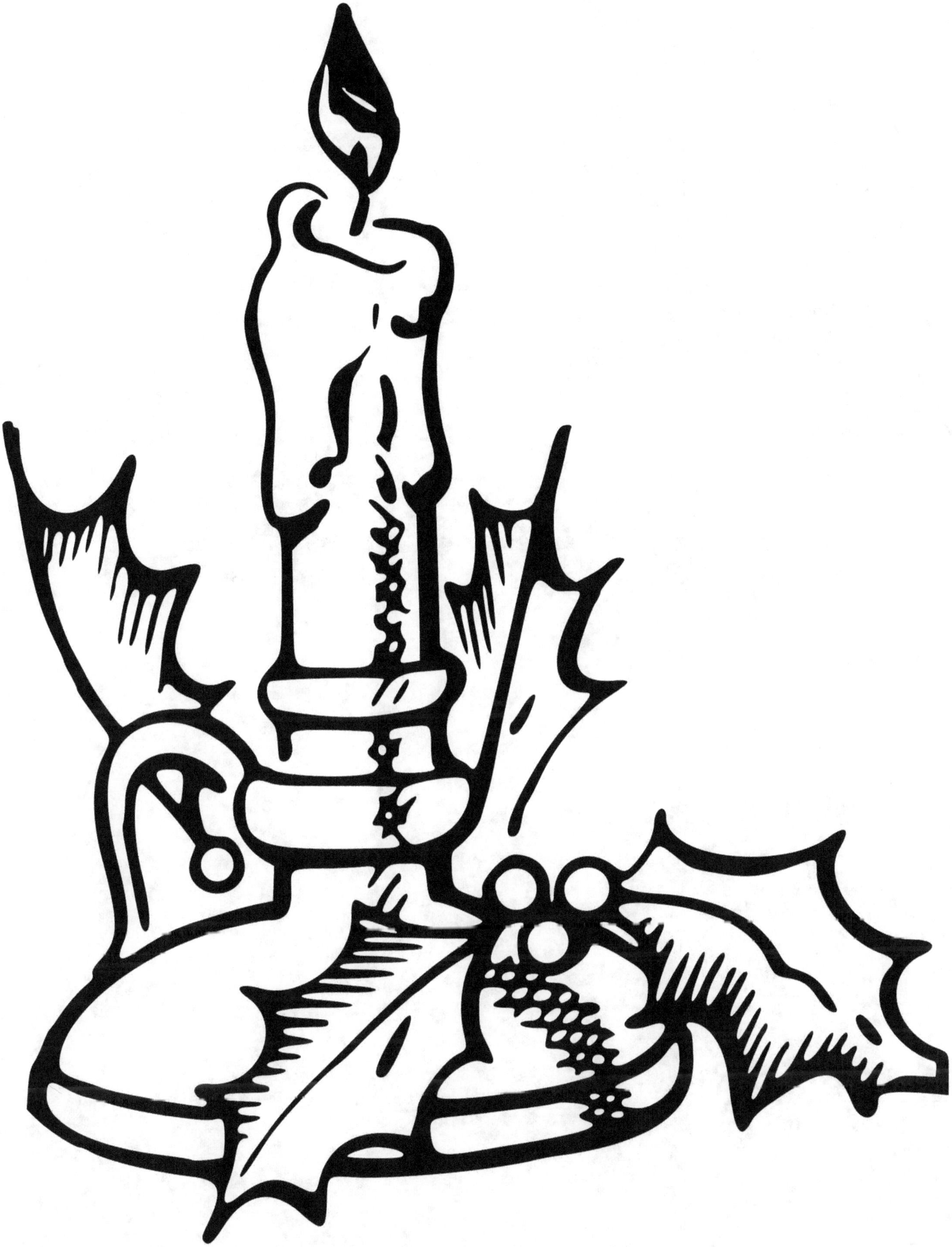

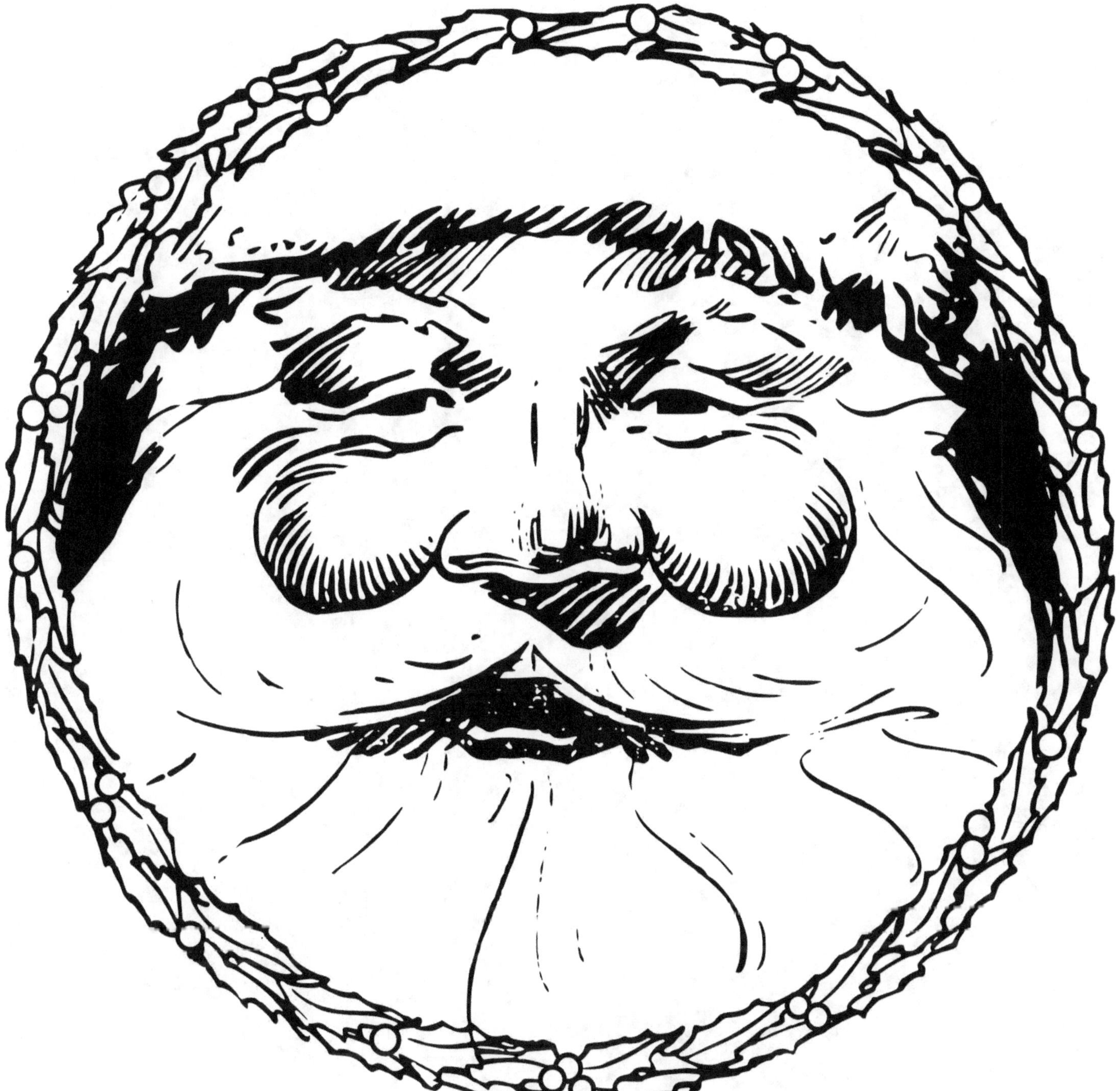

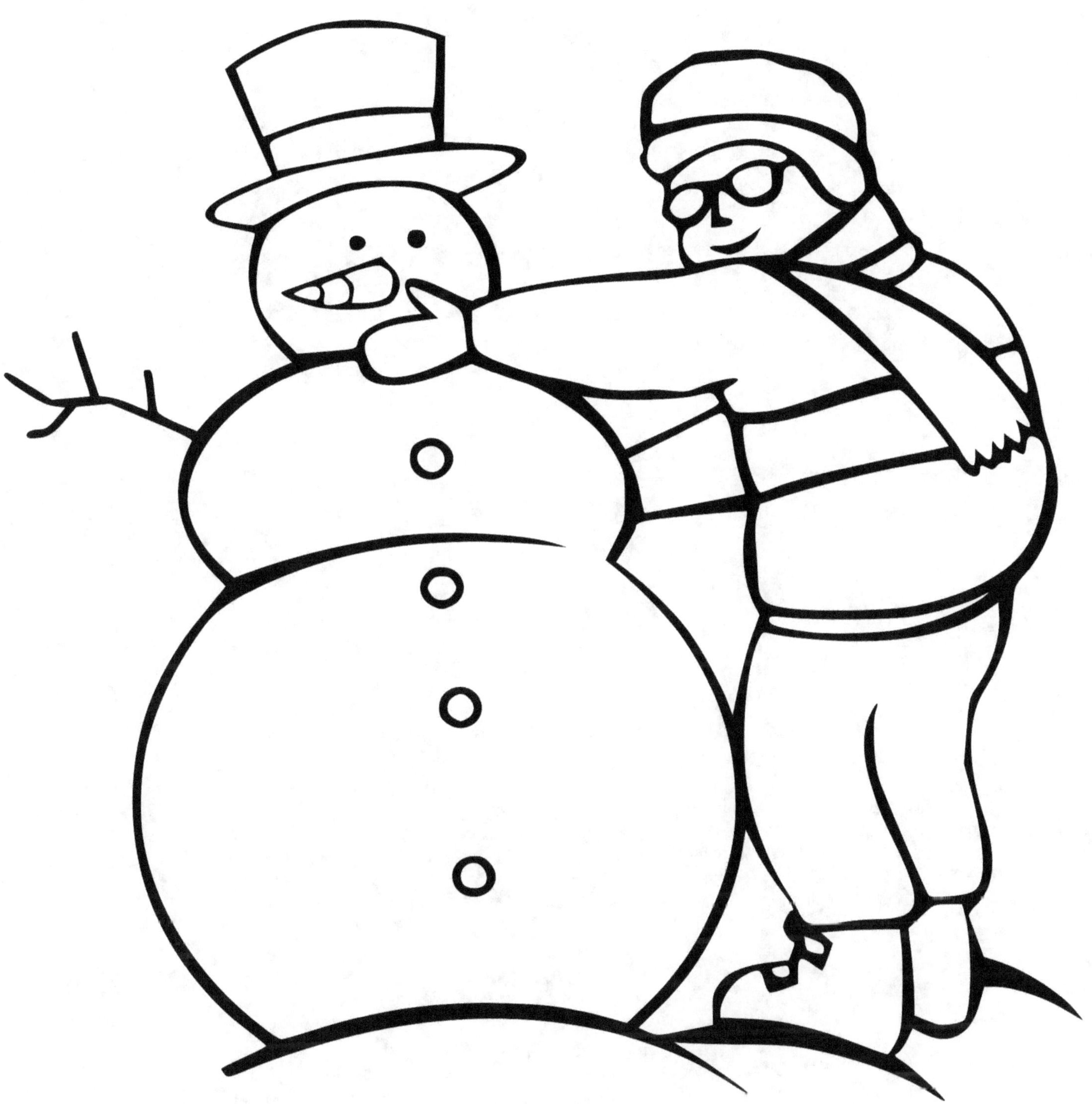

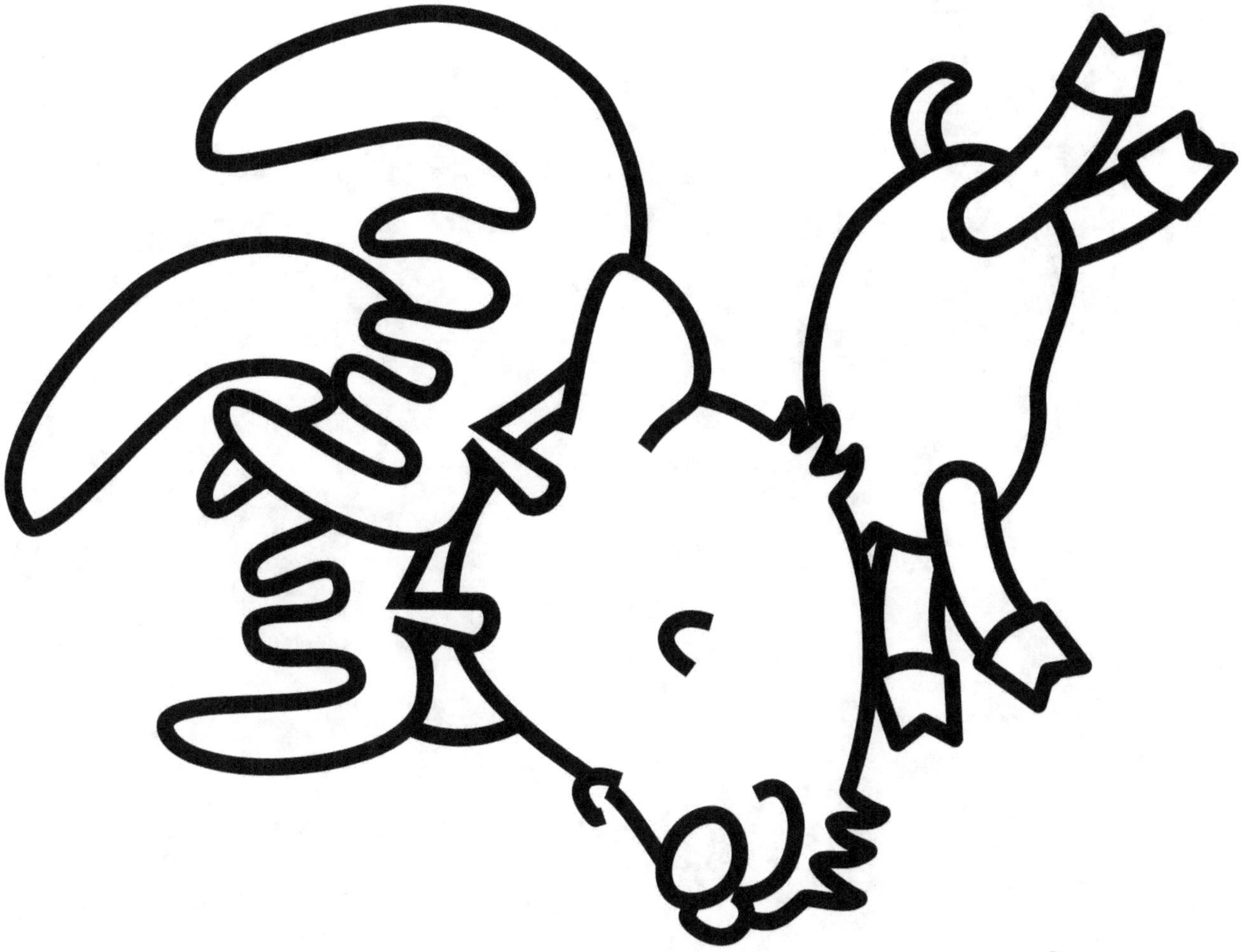

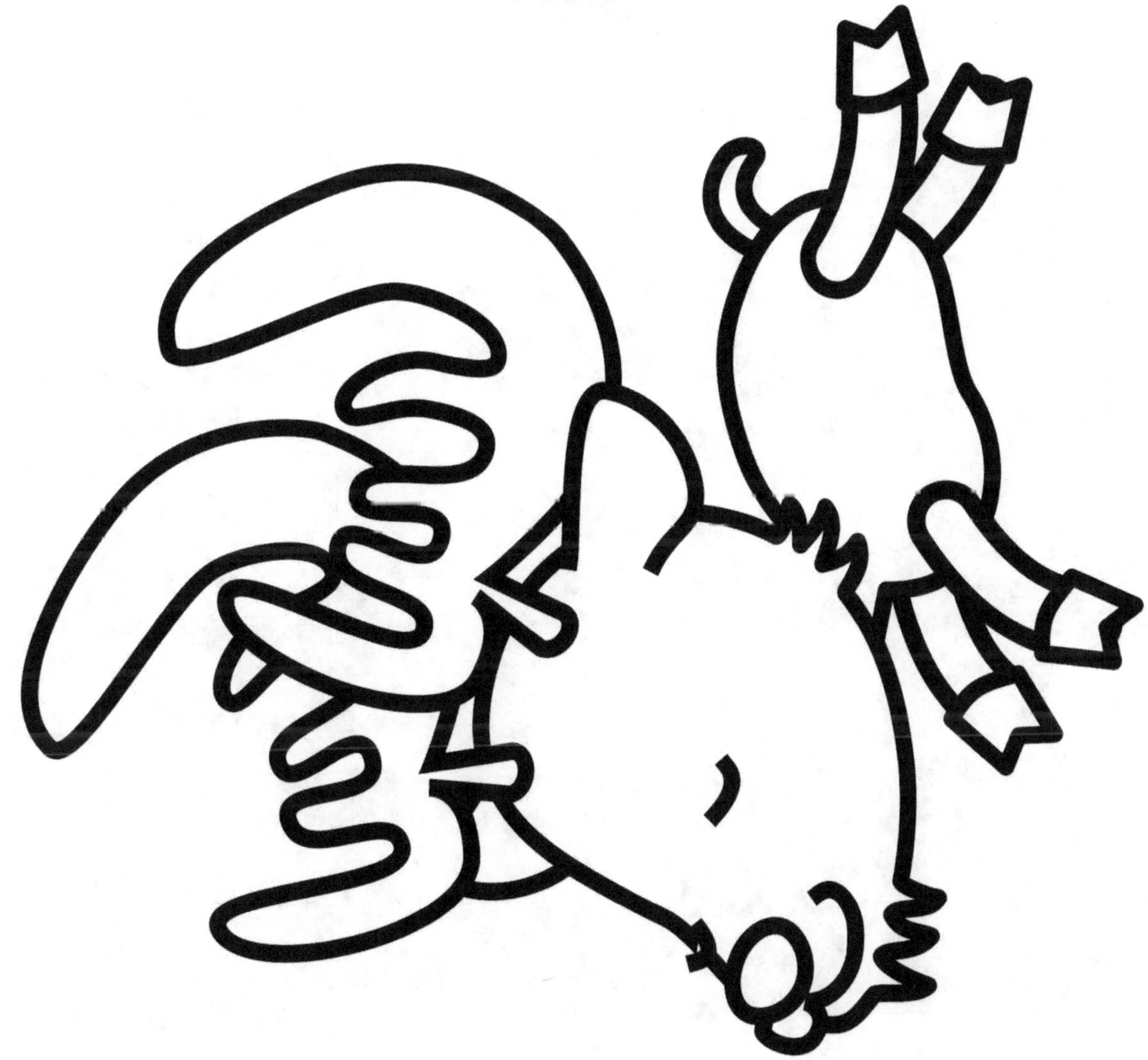

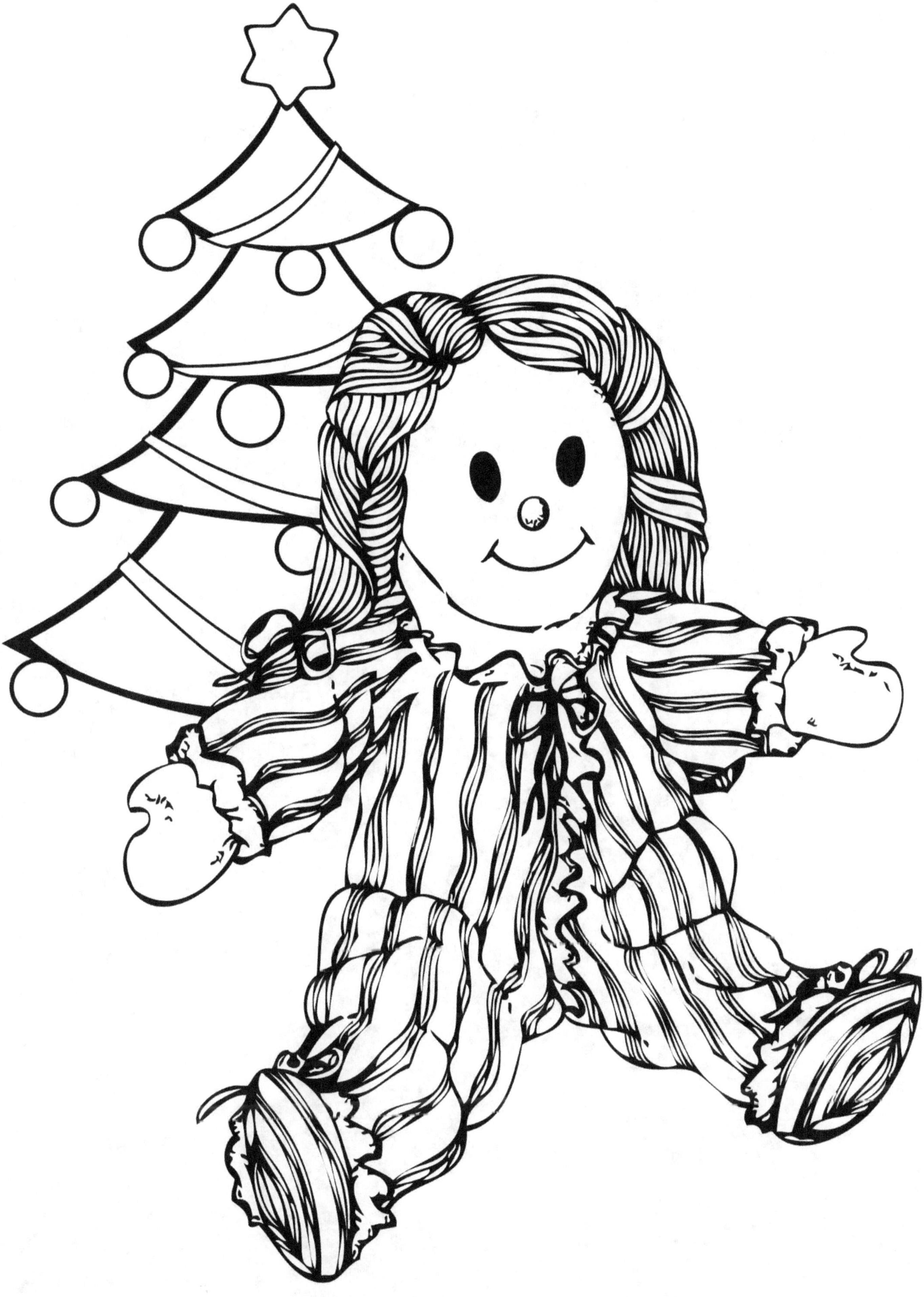

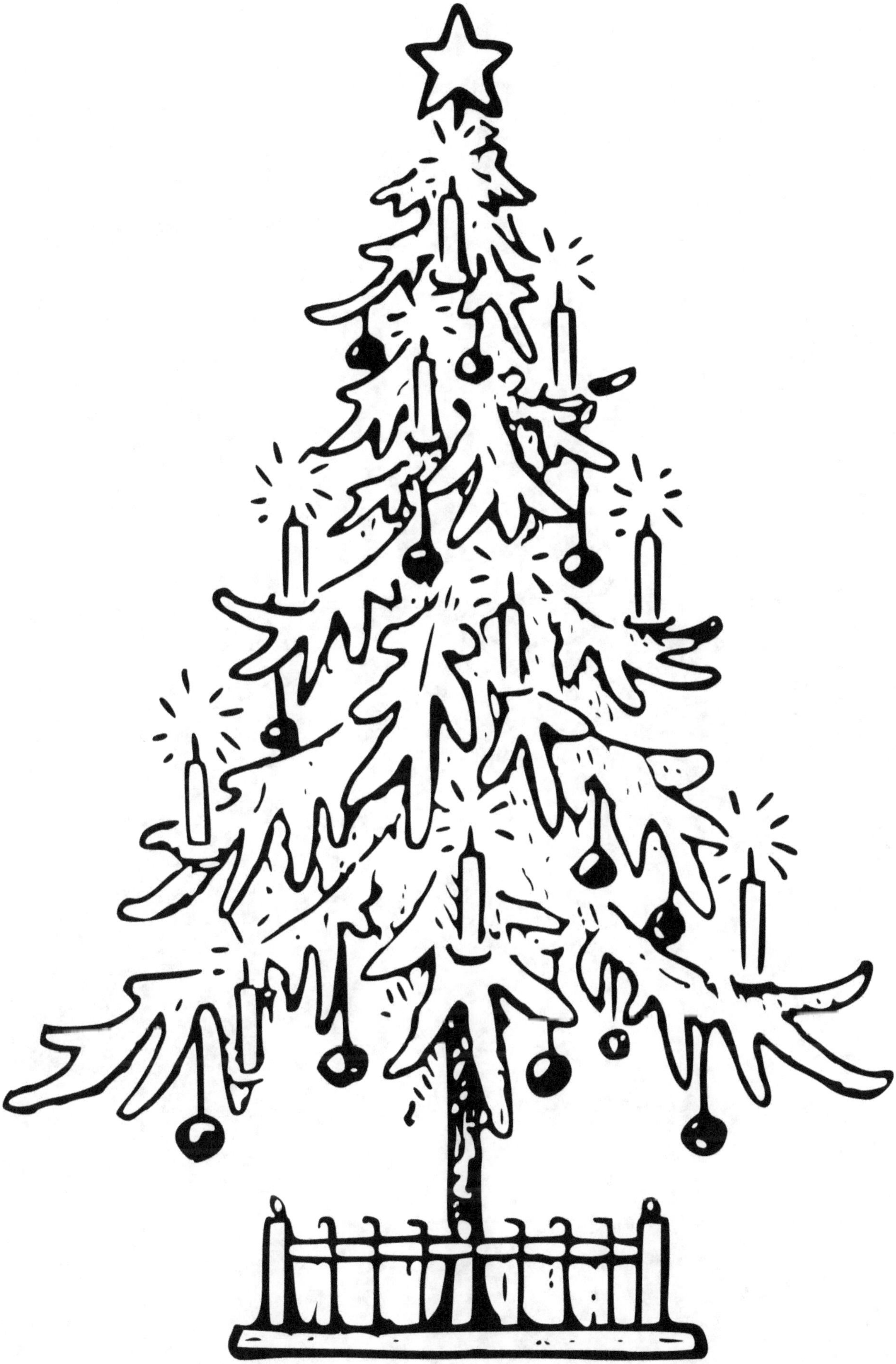

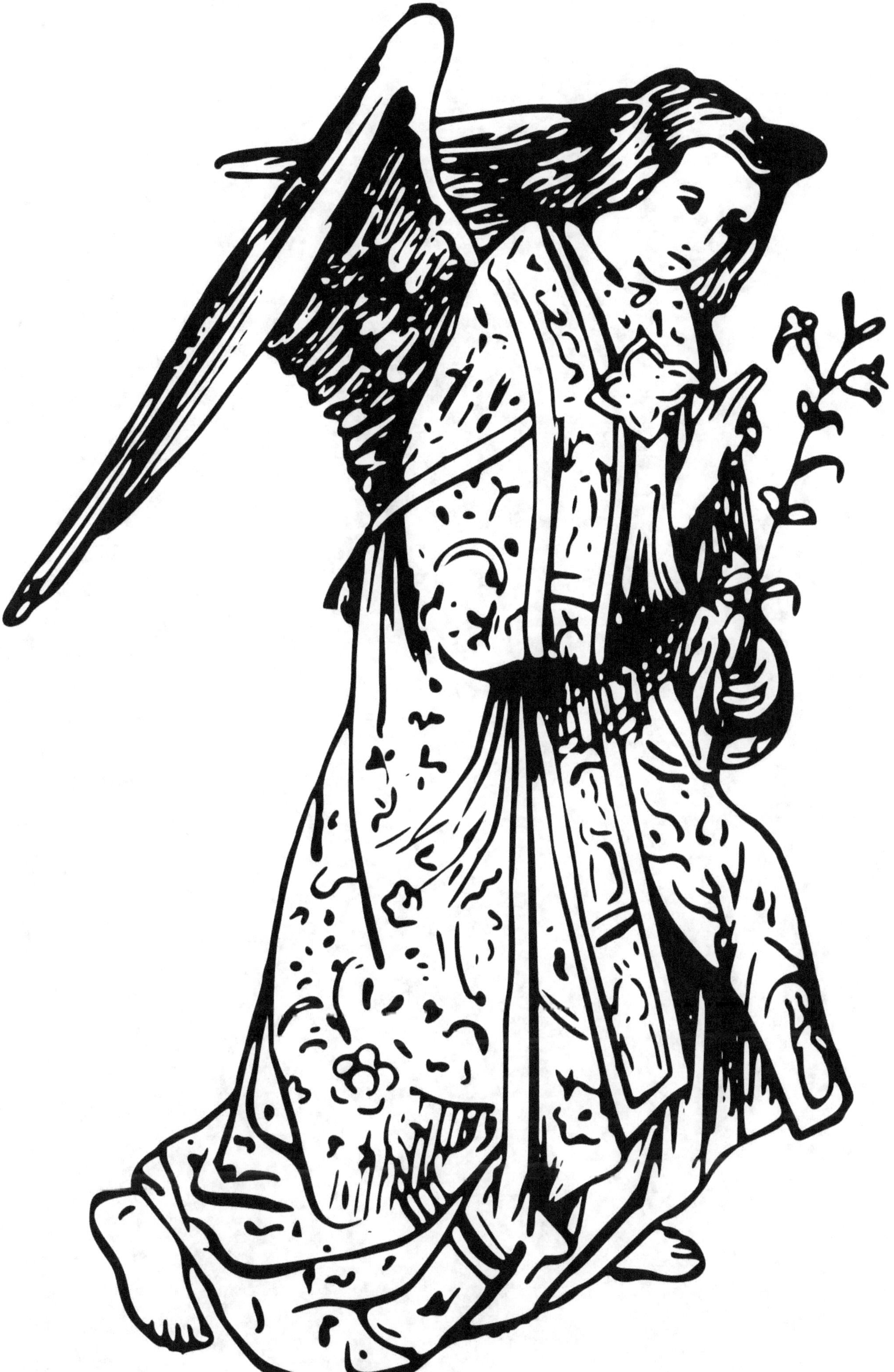

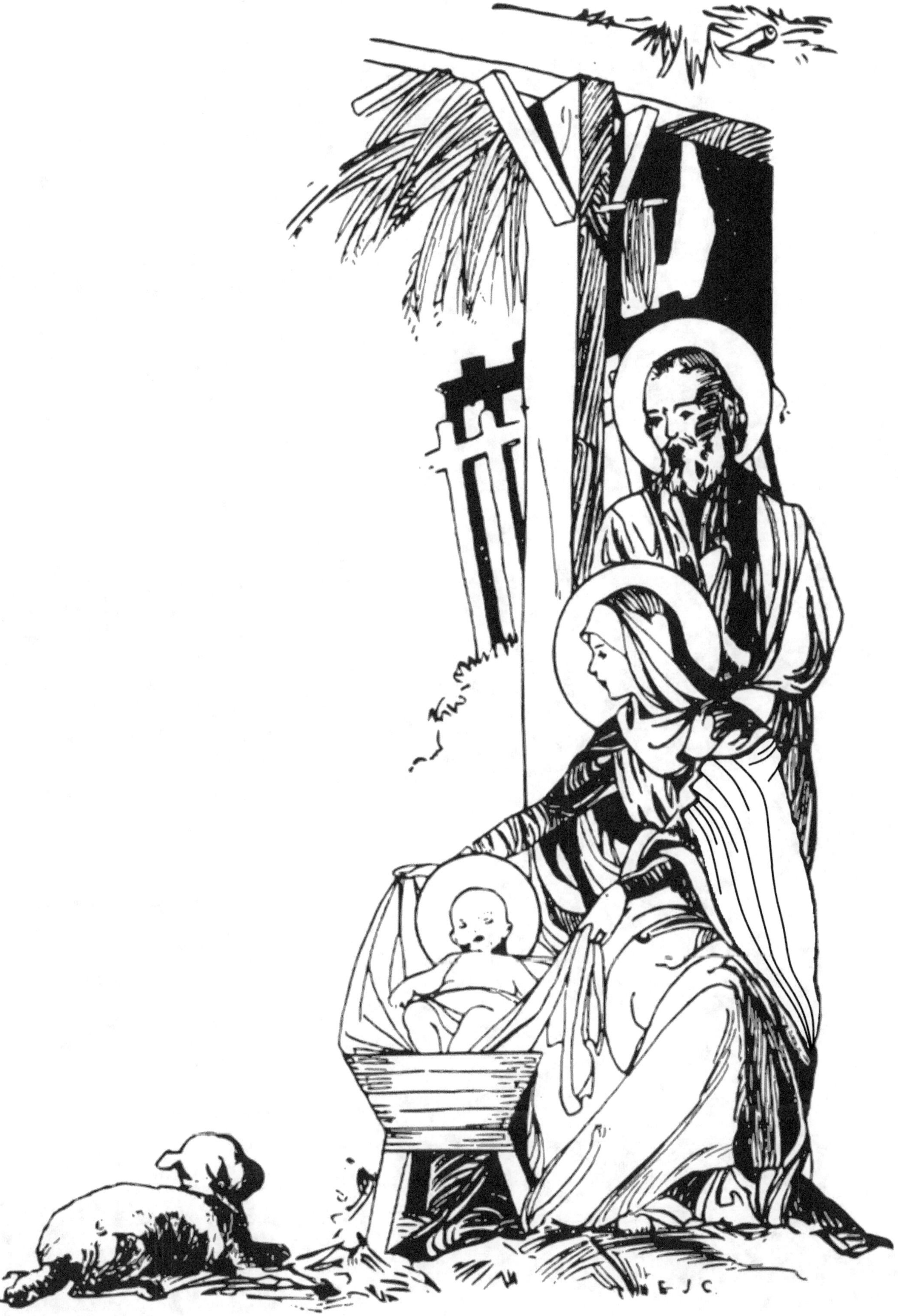

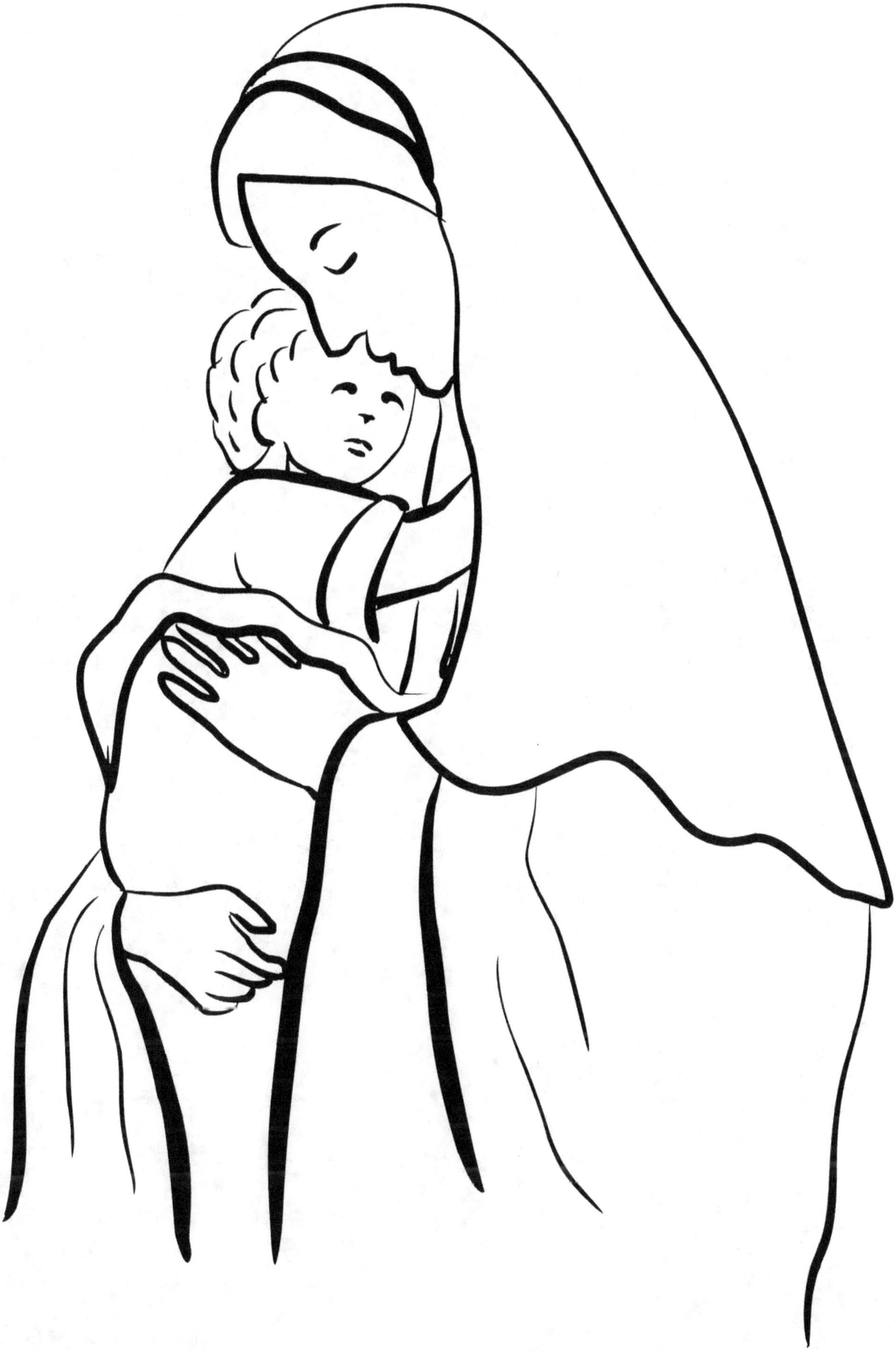

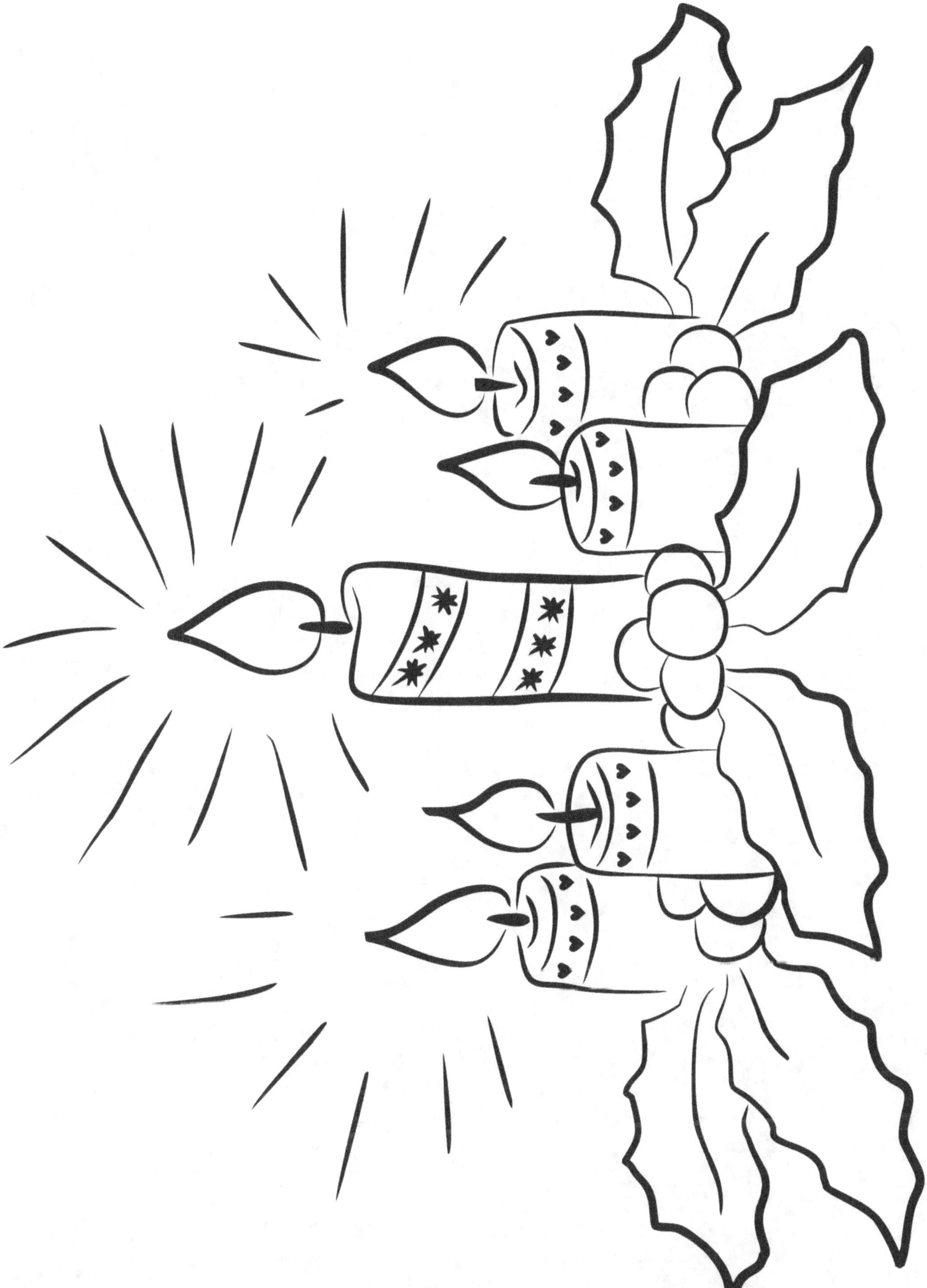

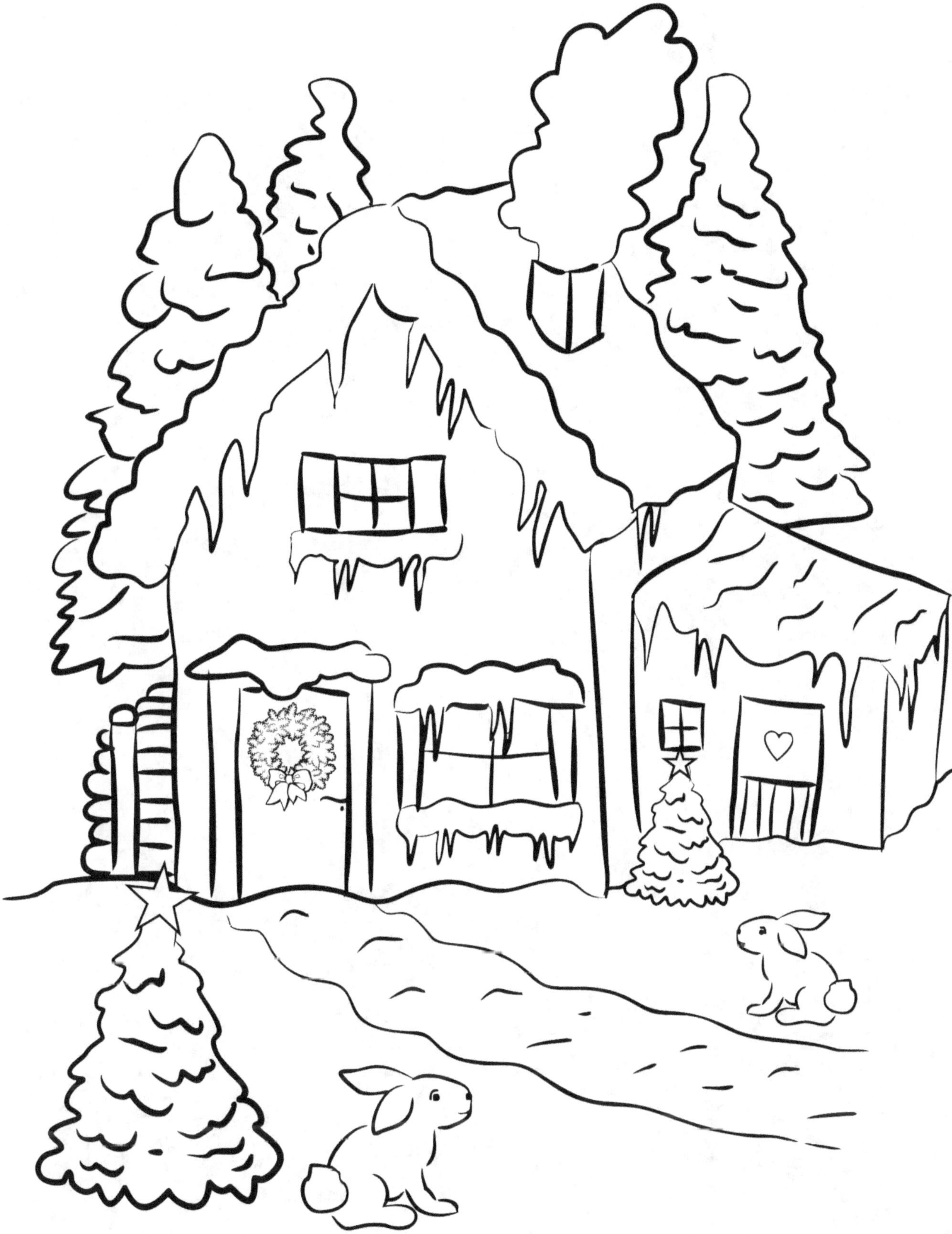

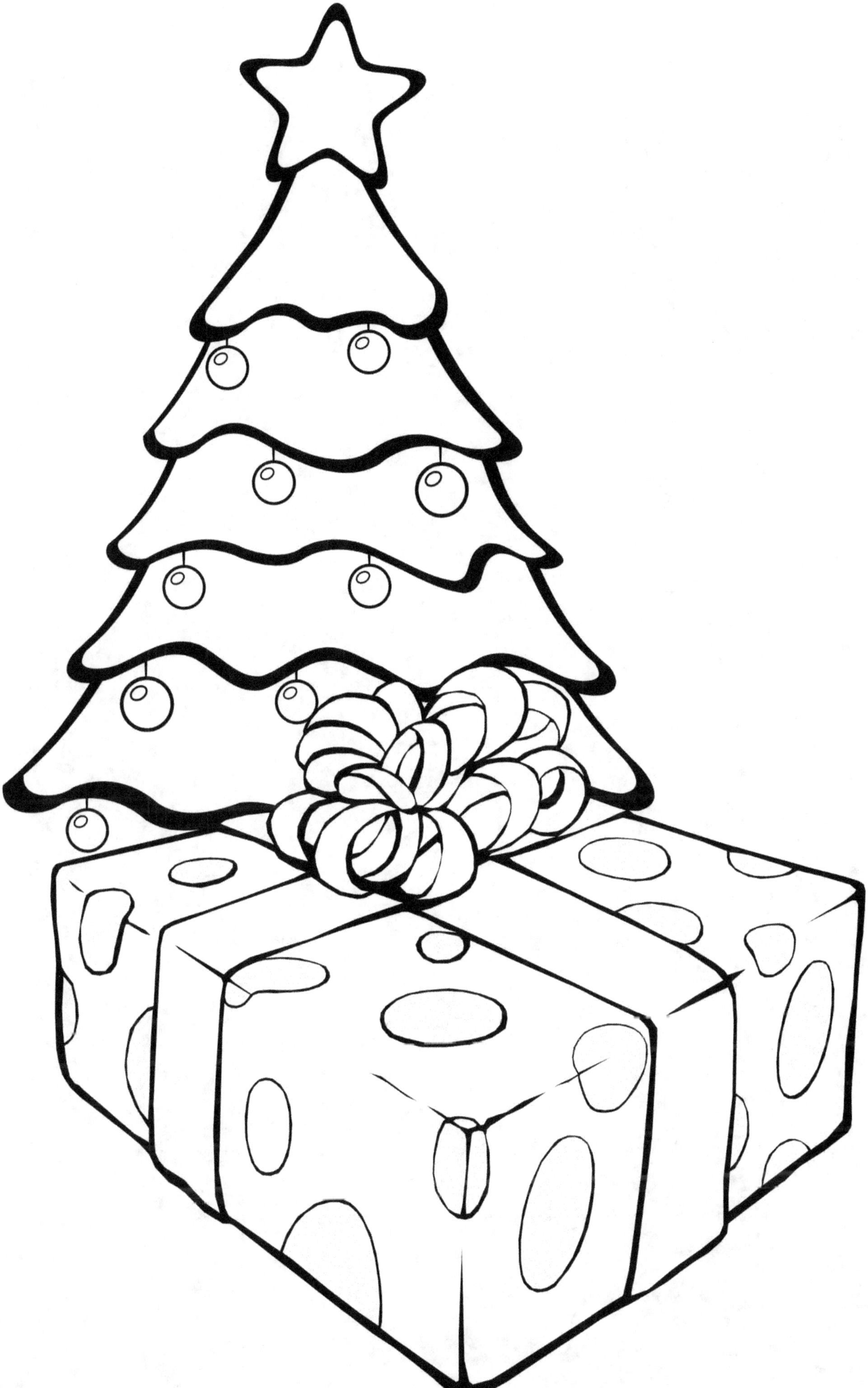

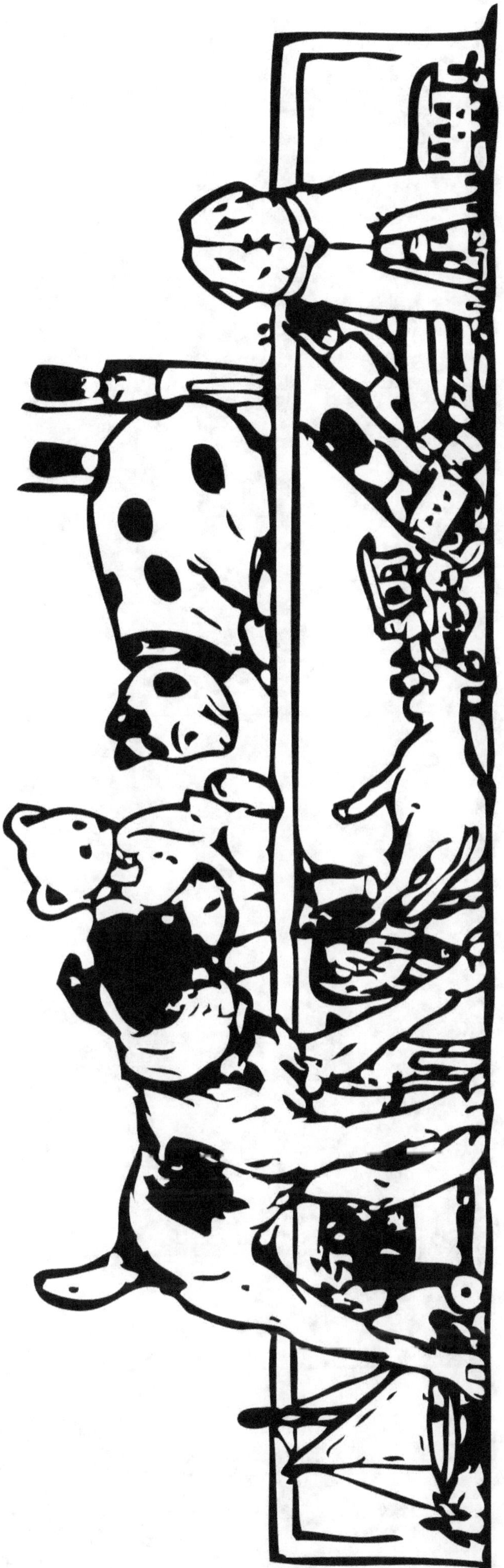

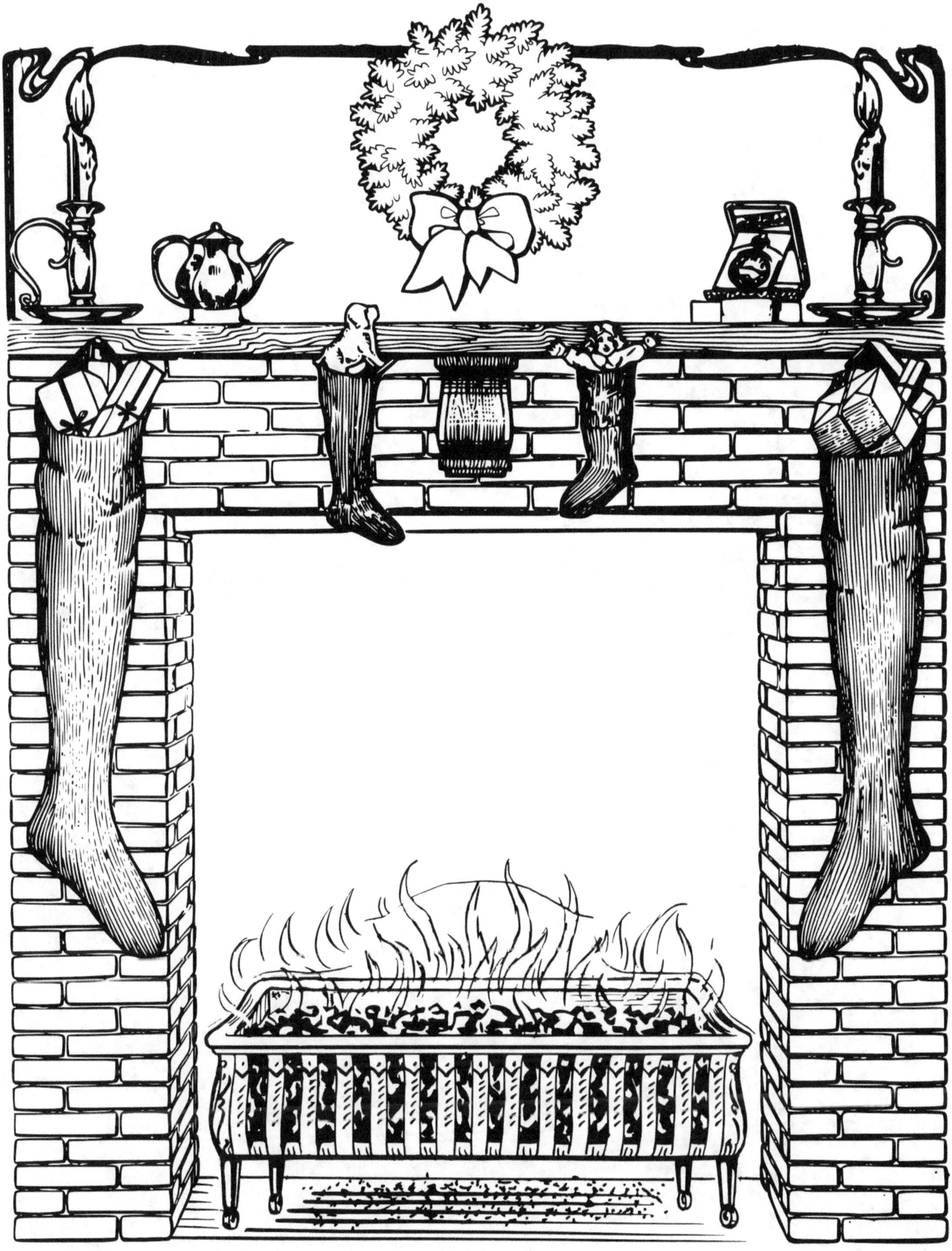

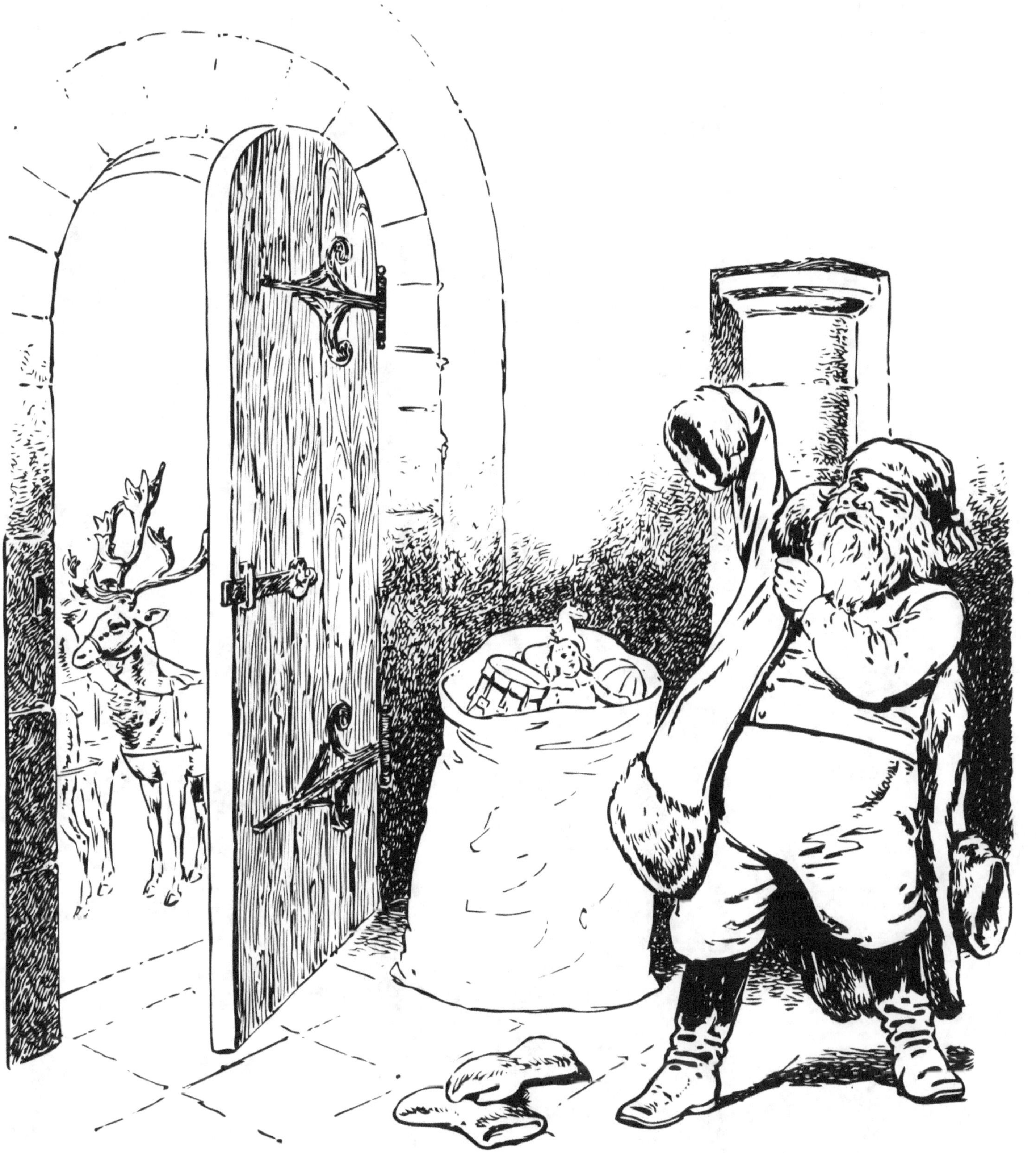

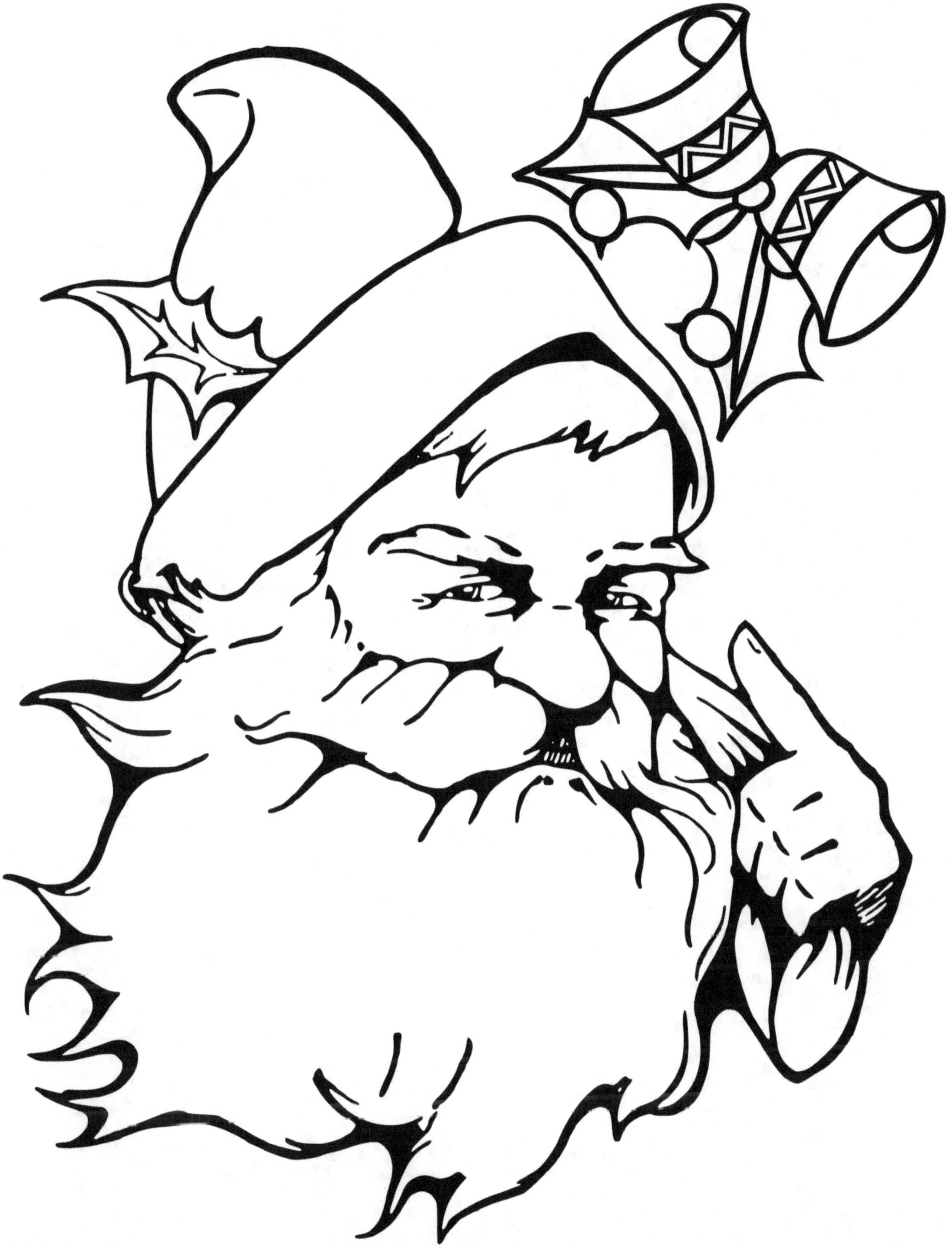

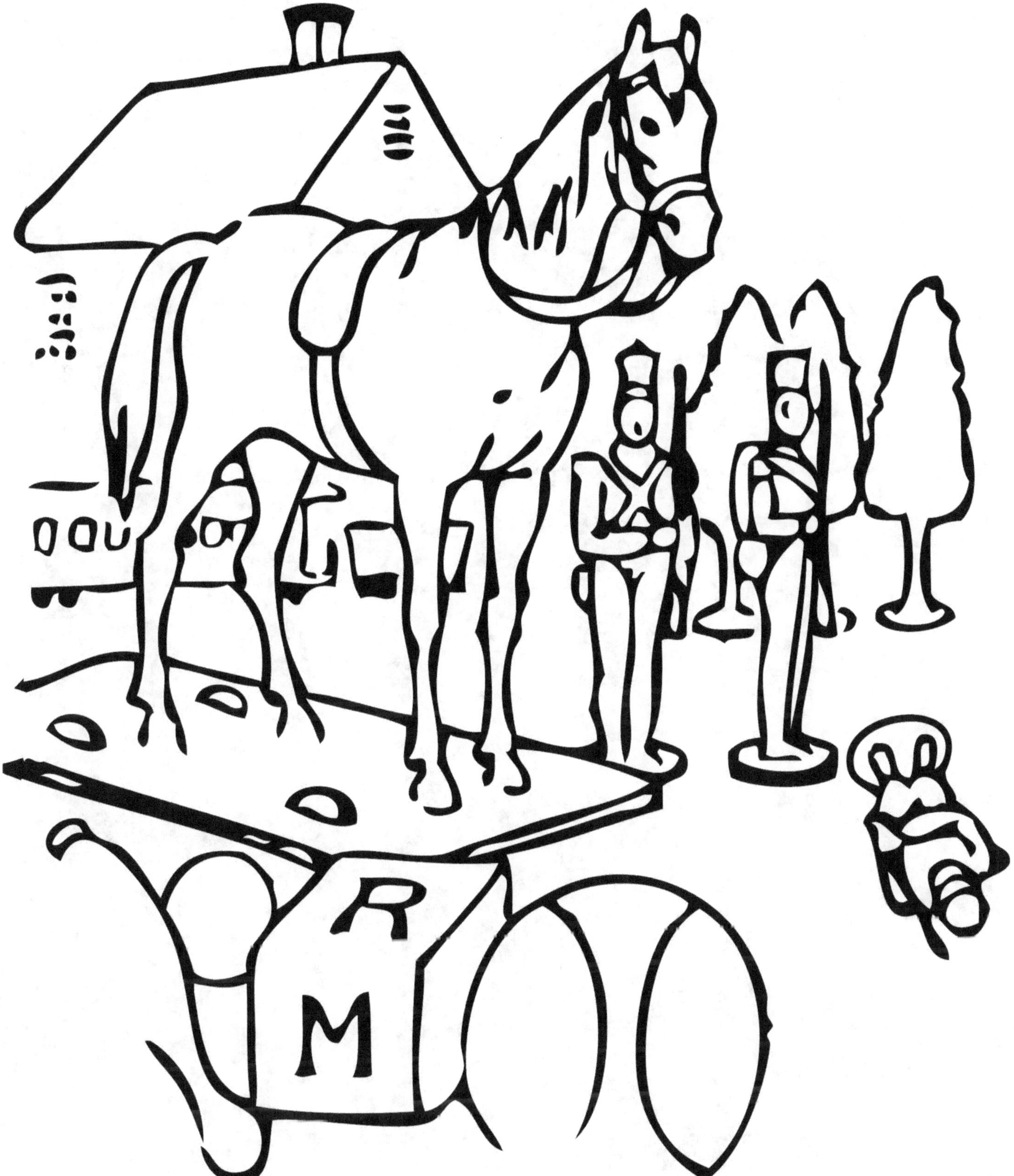
R
M

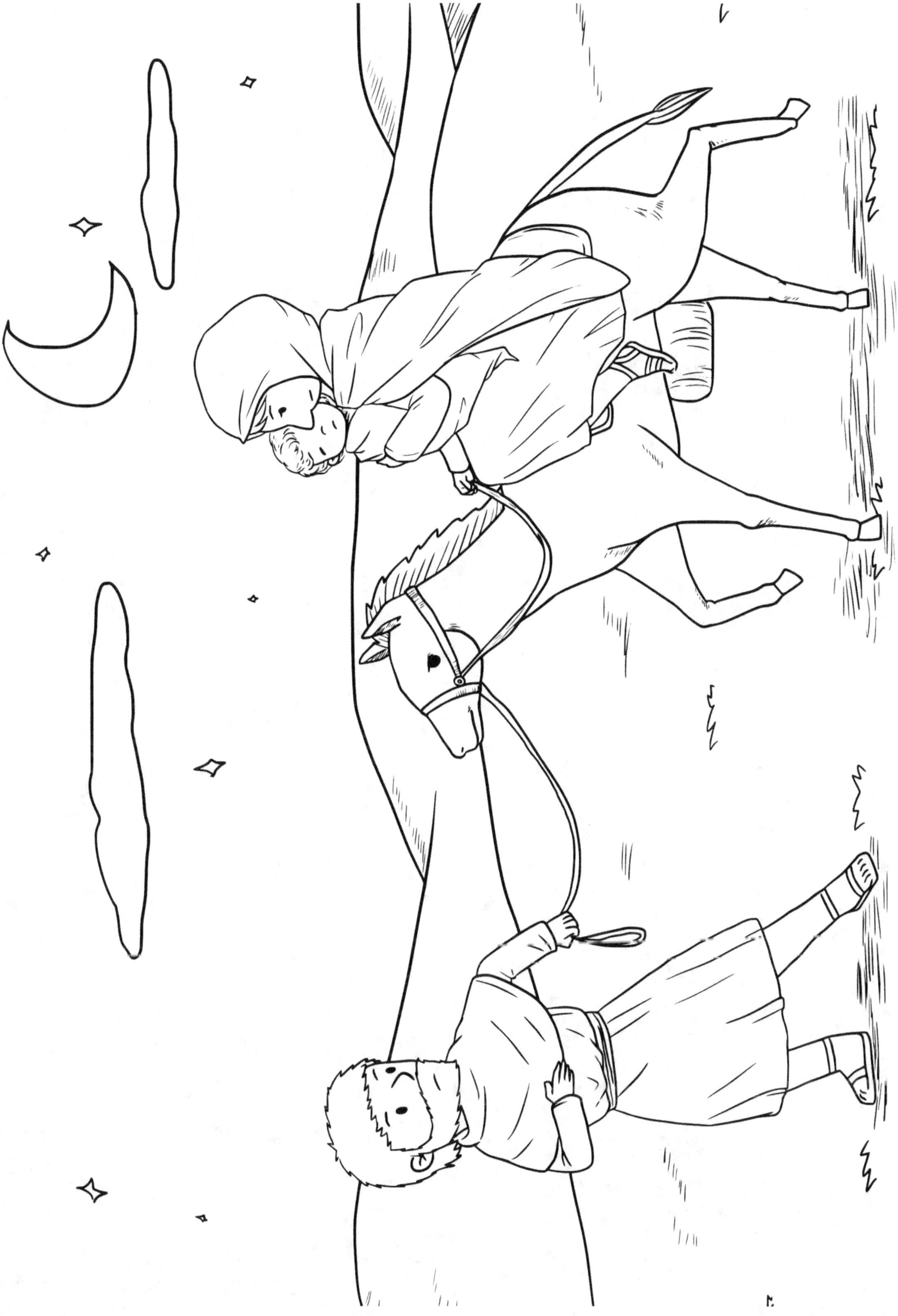

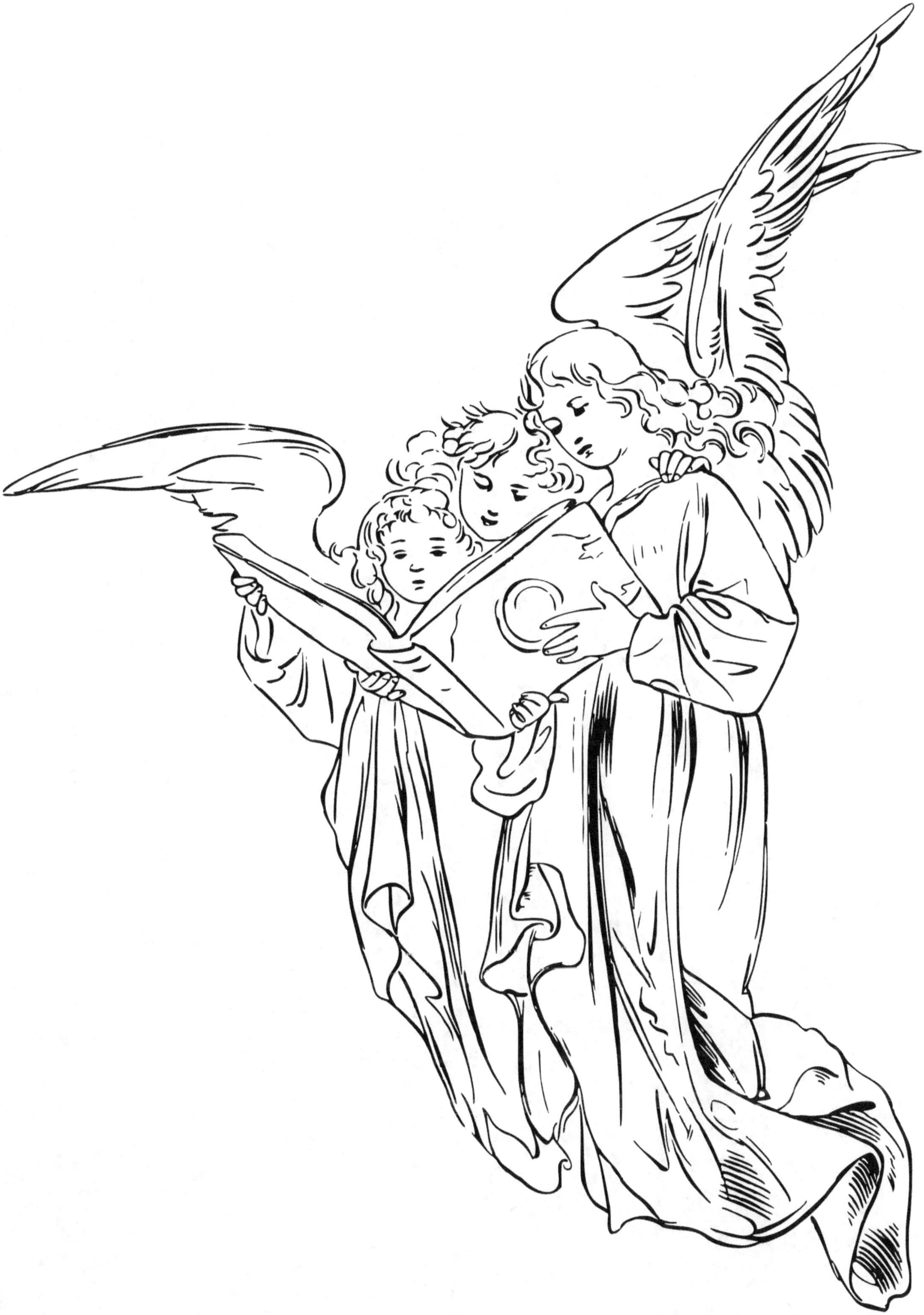

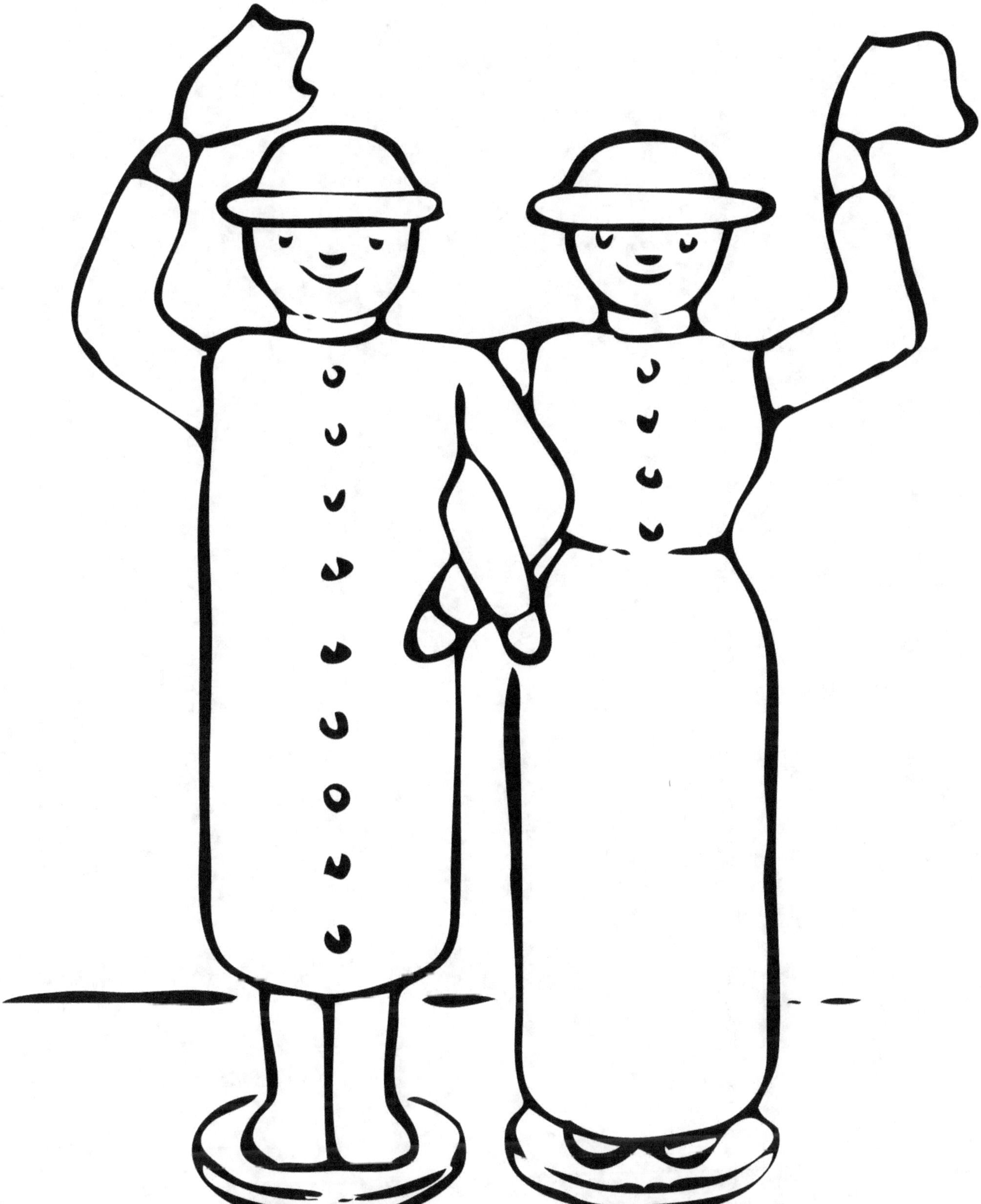

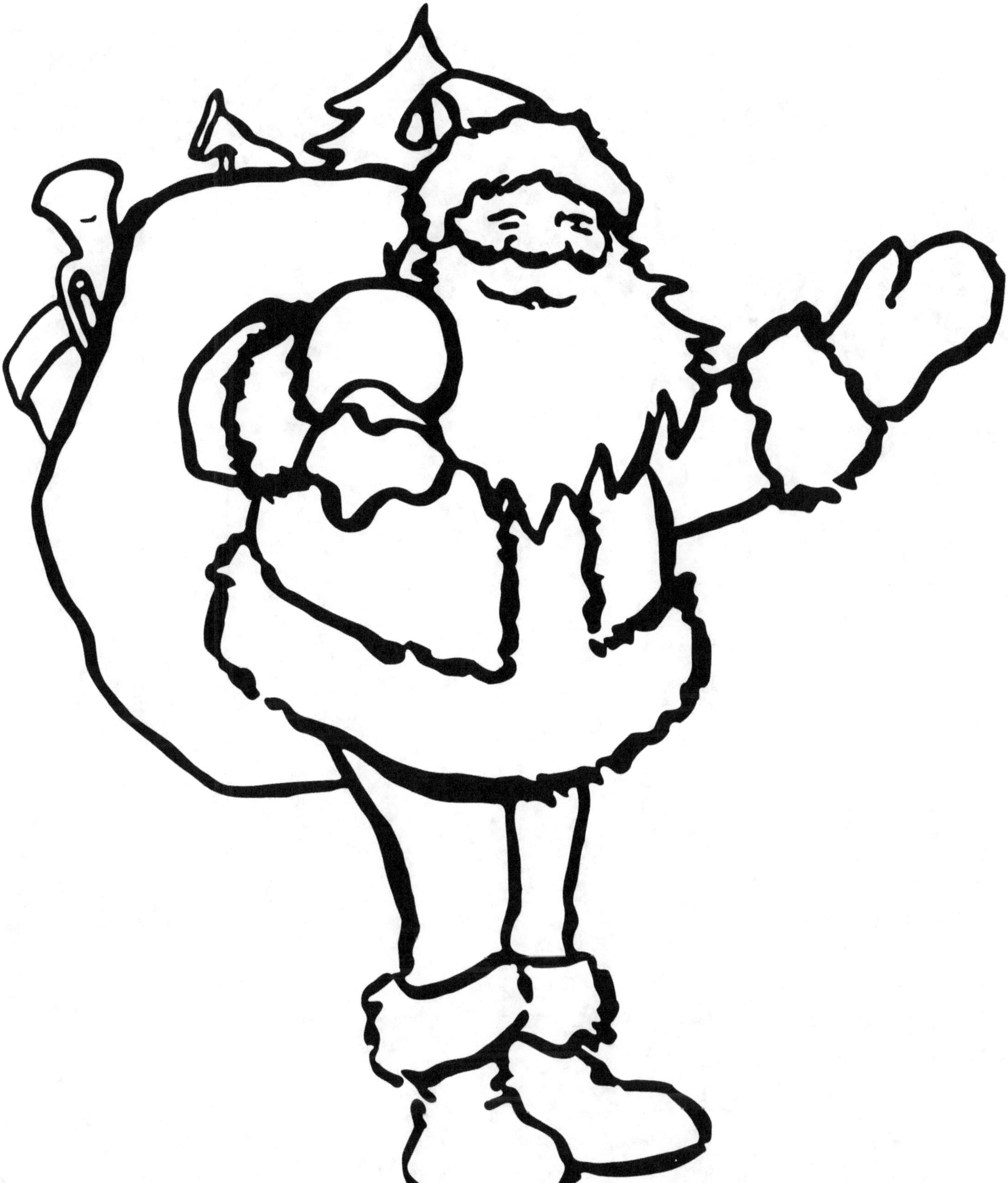

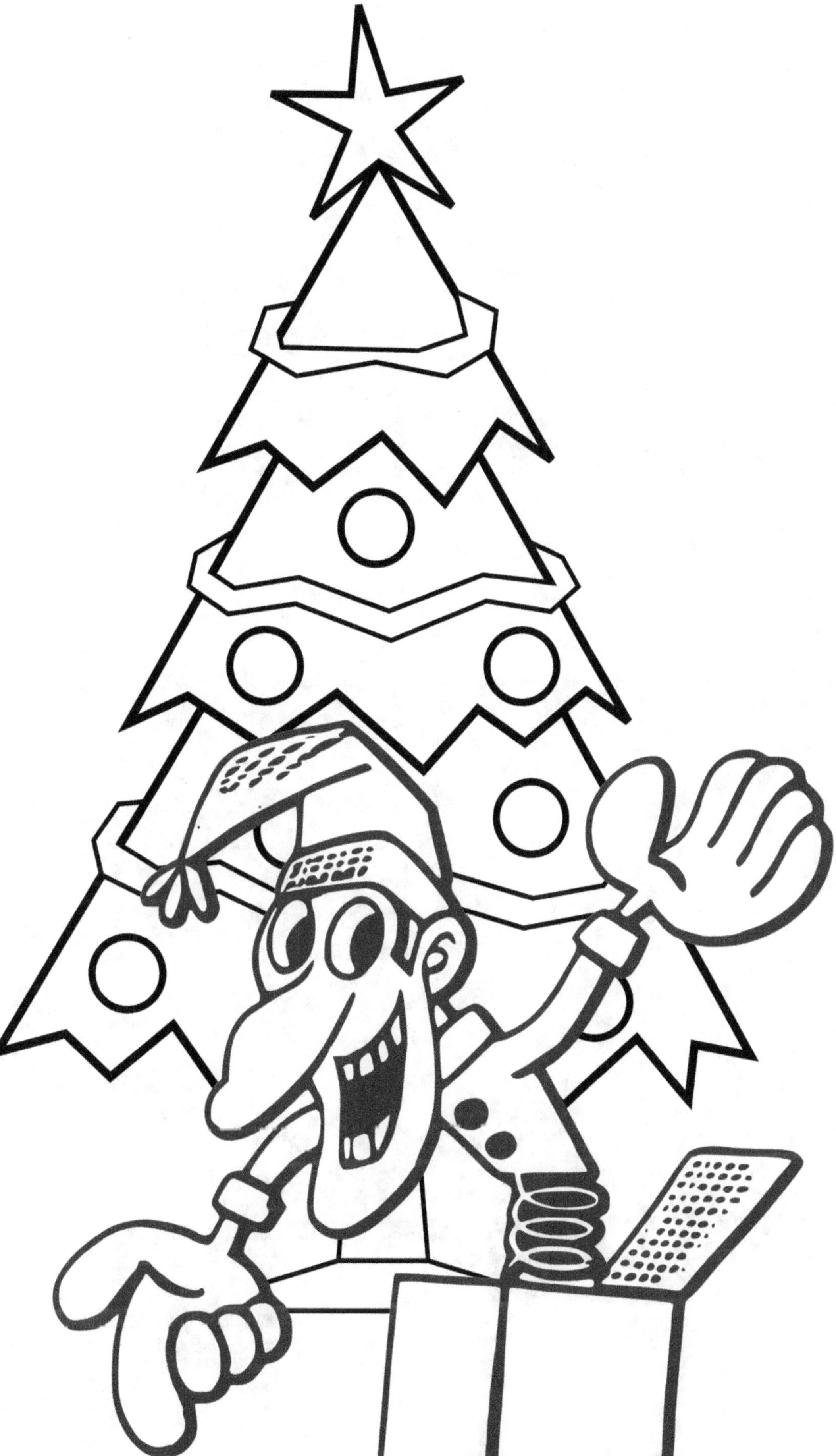

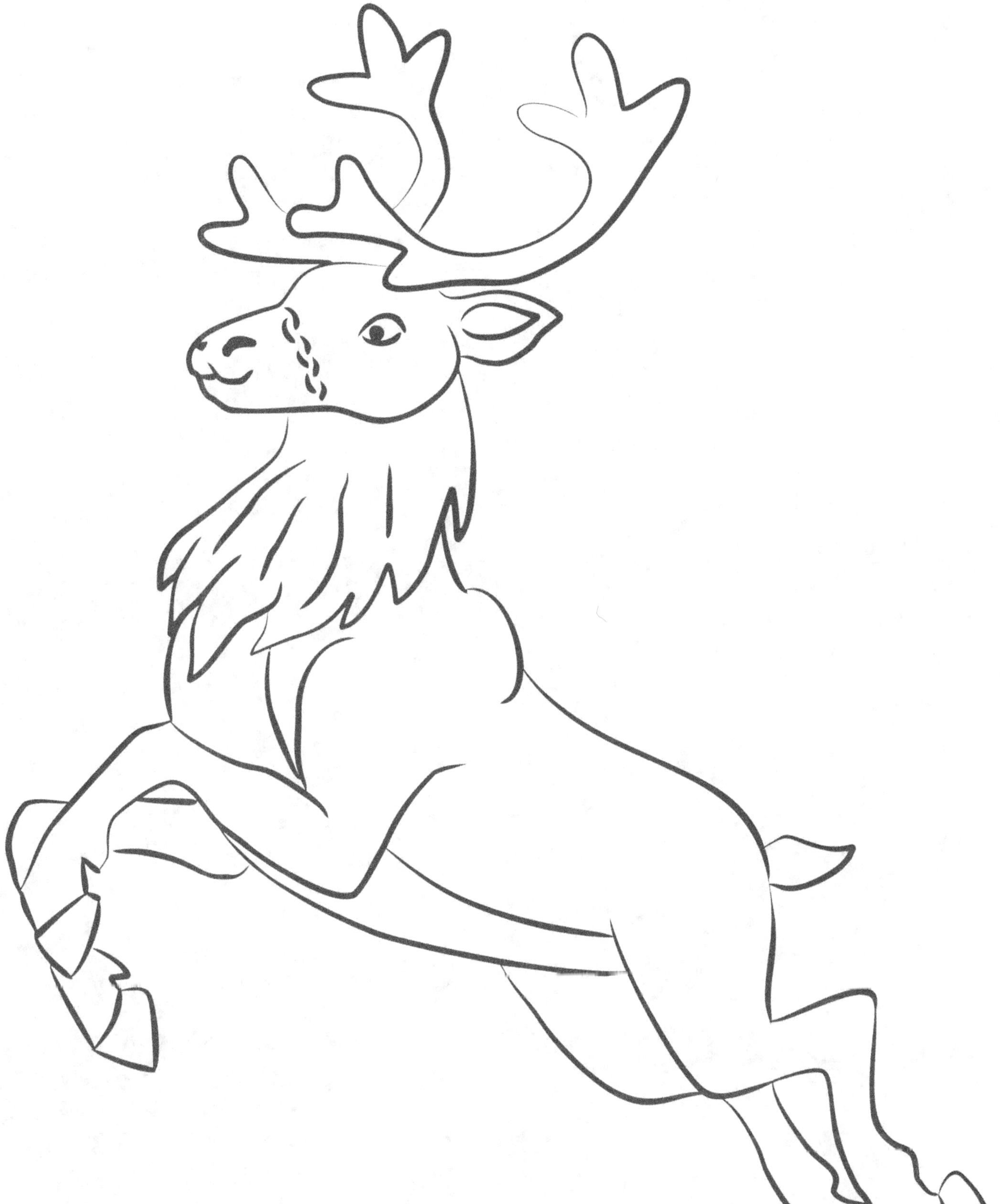

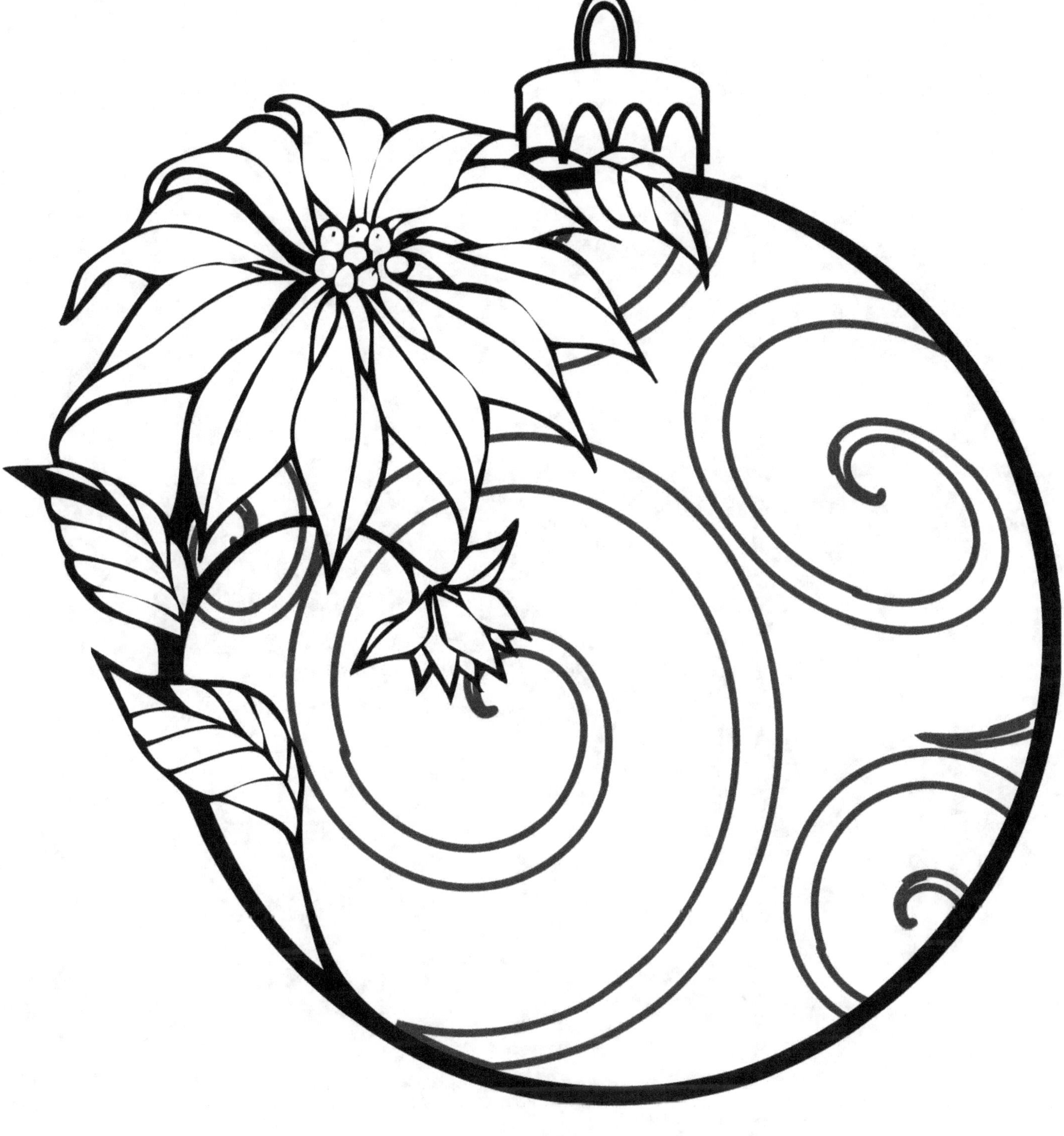

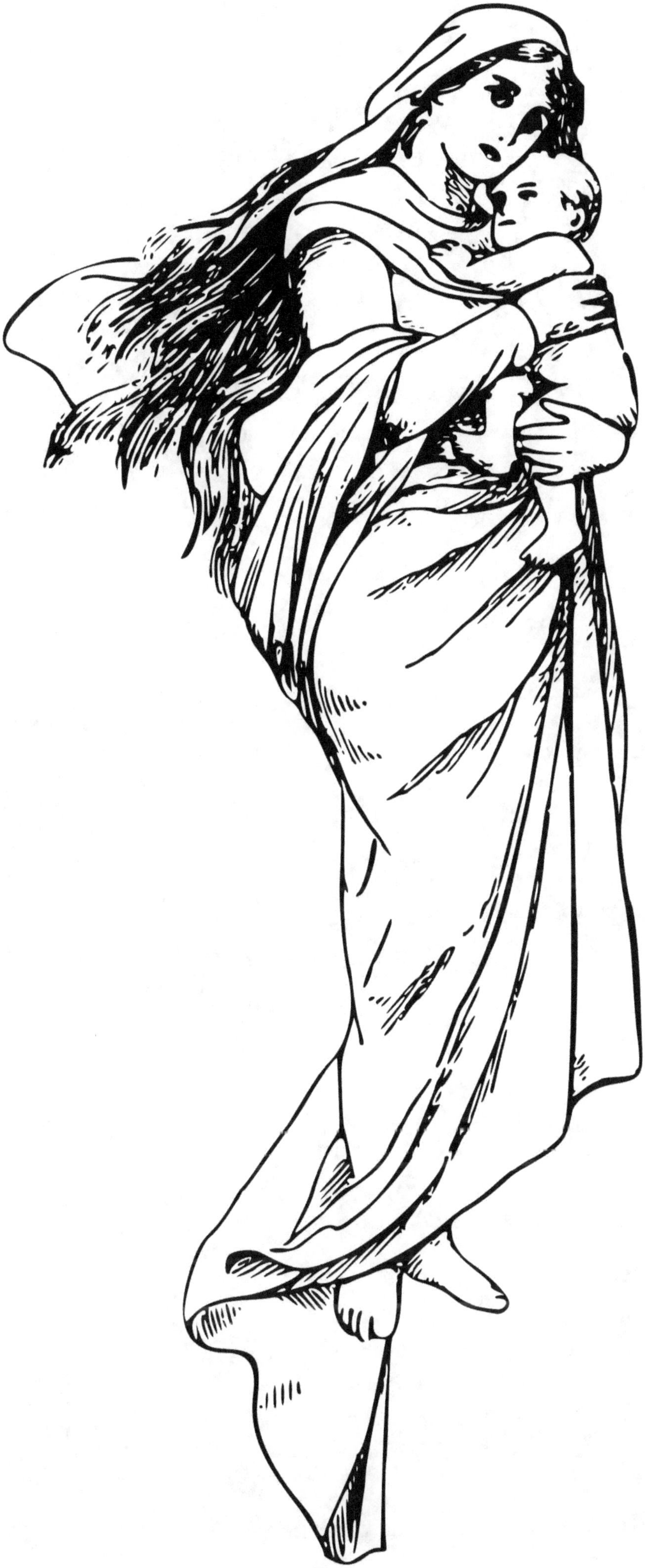

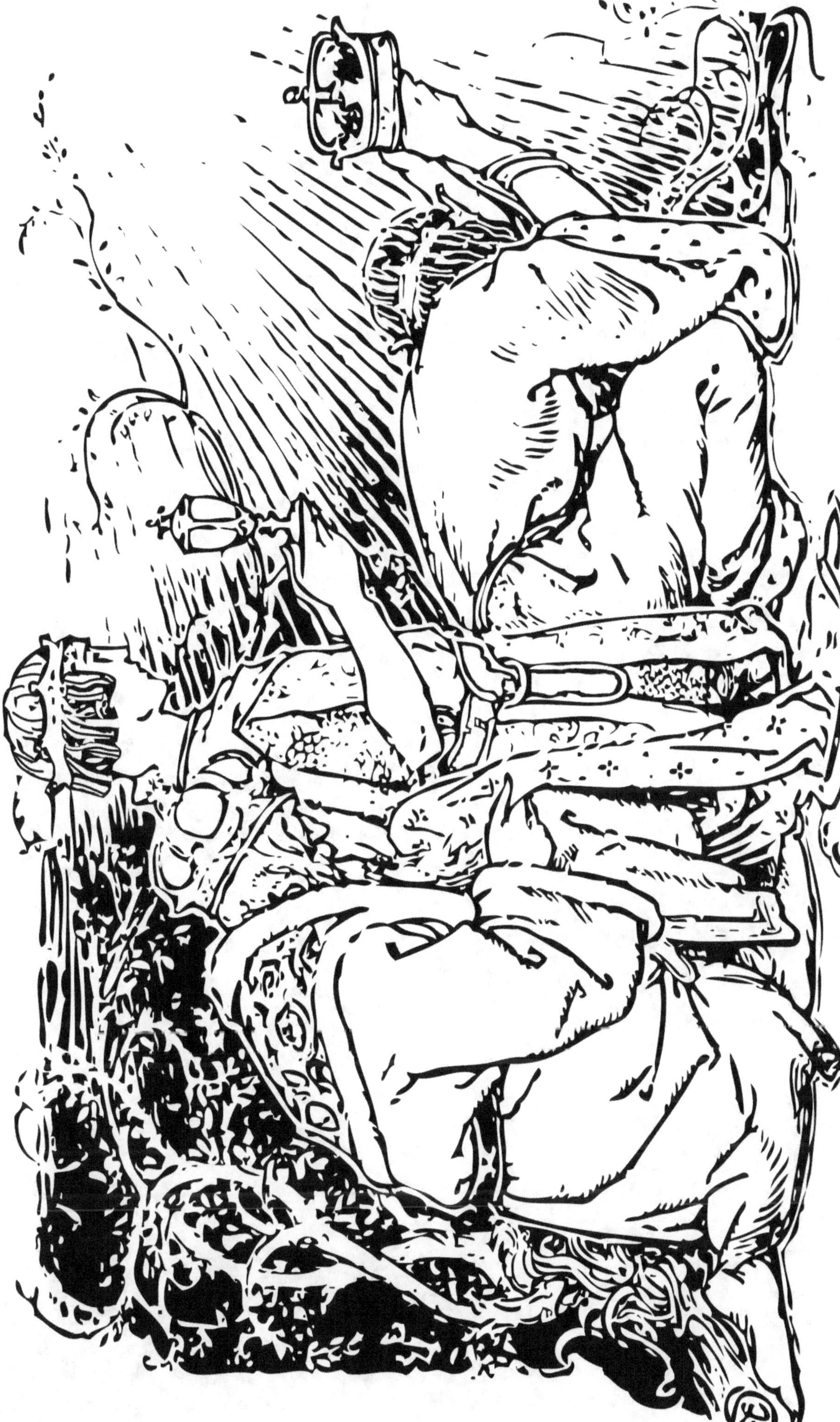

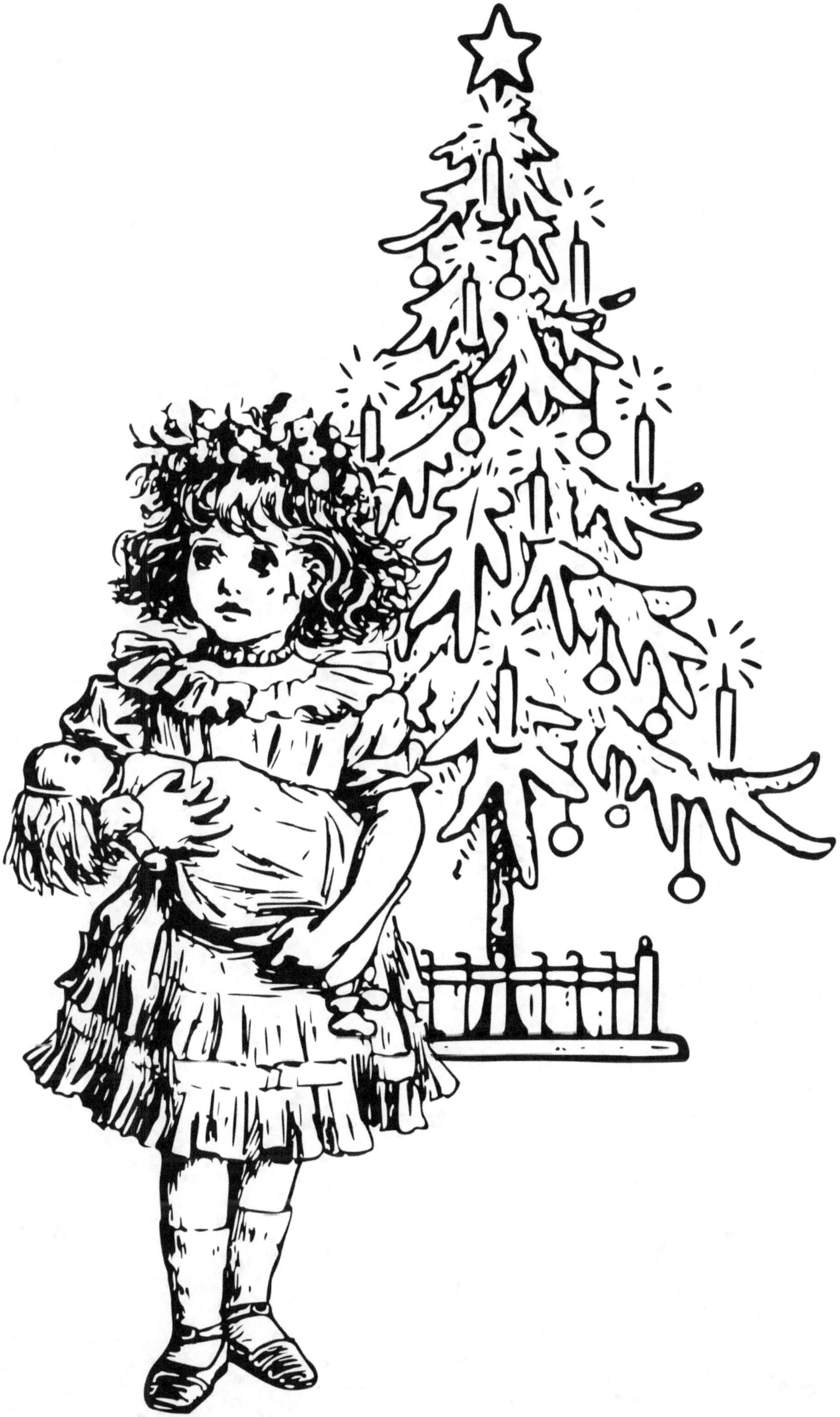

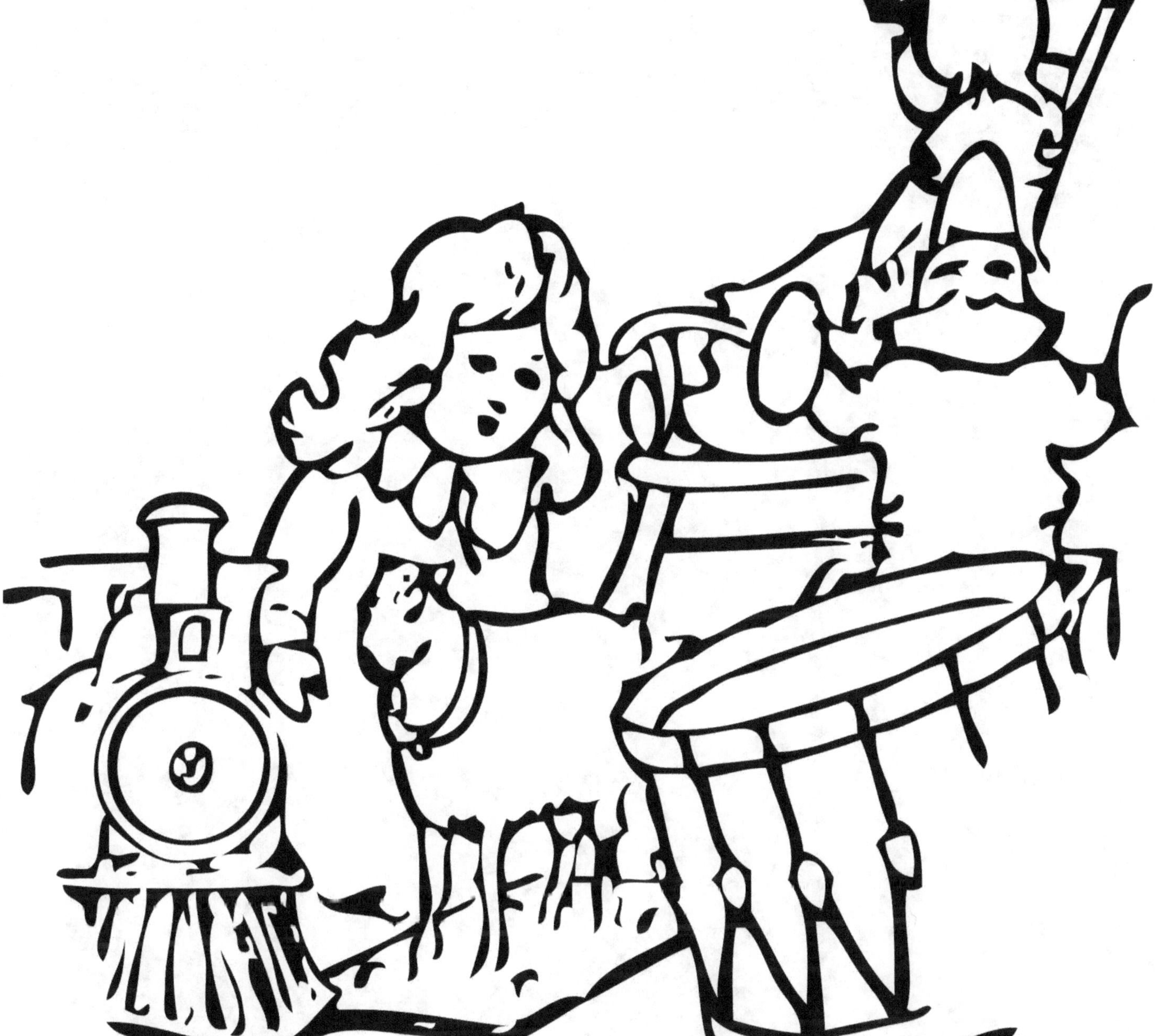

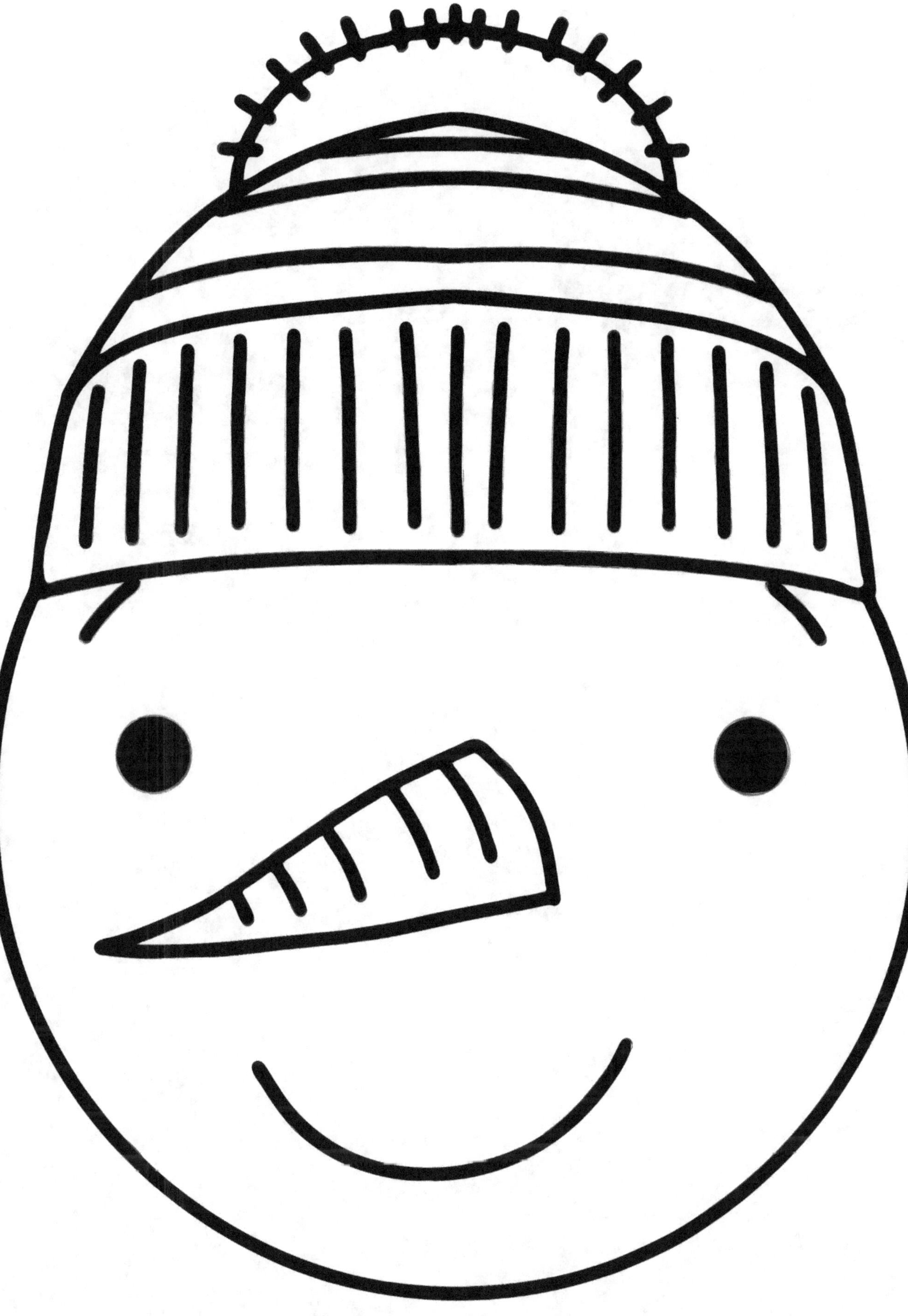

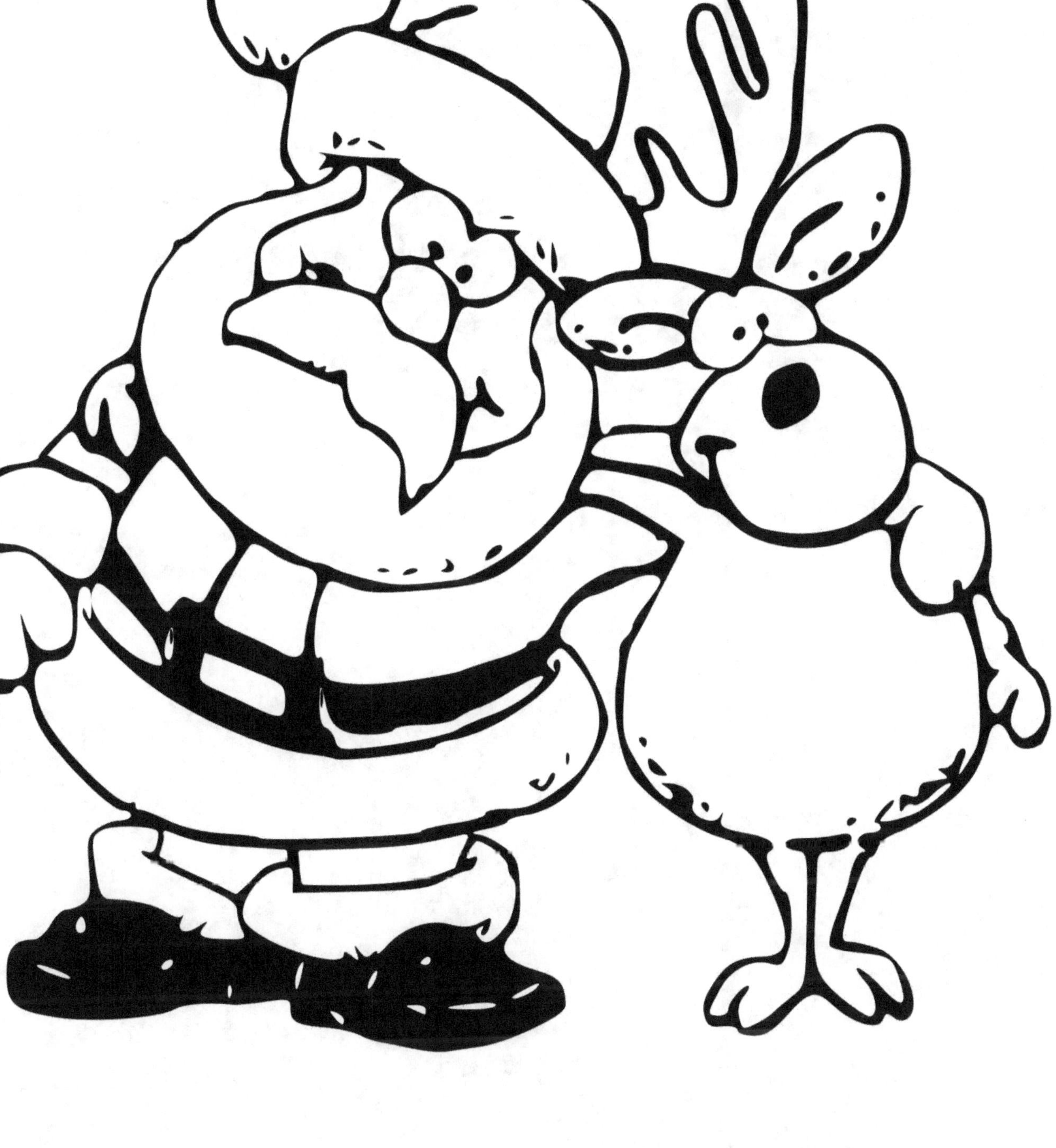

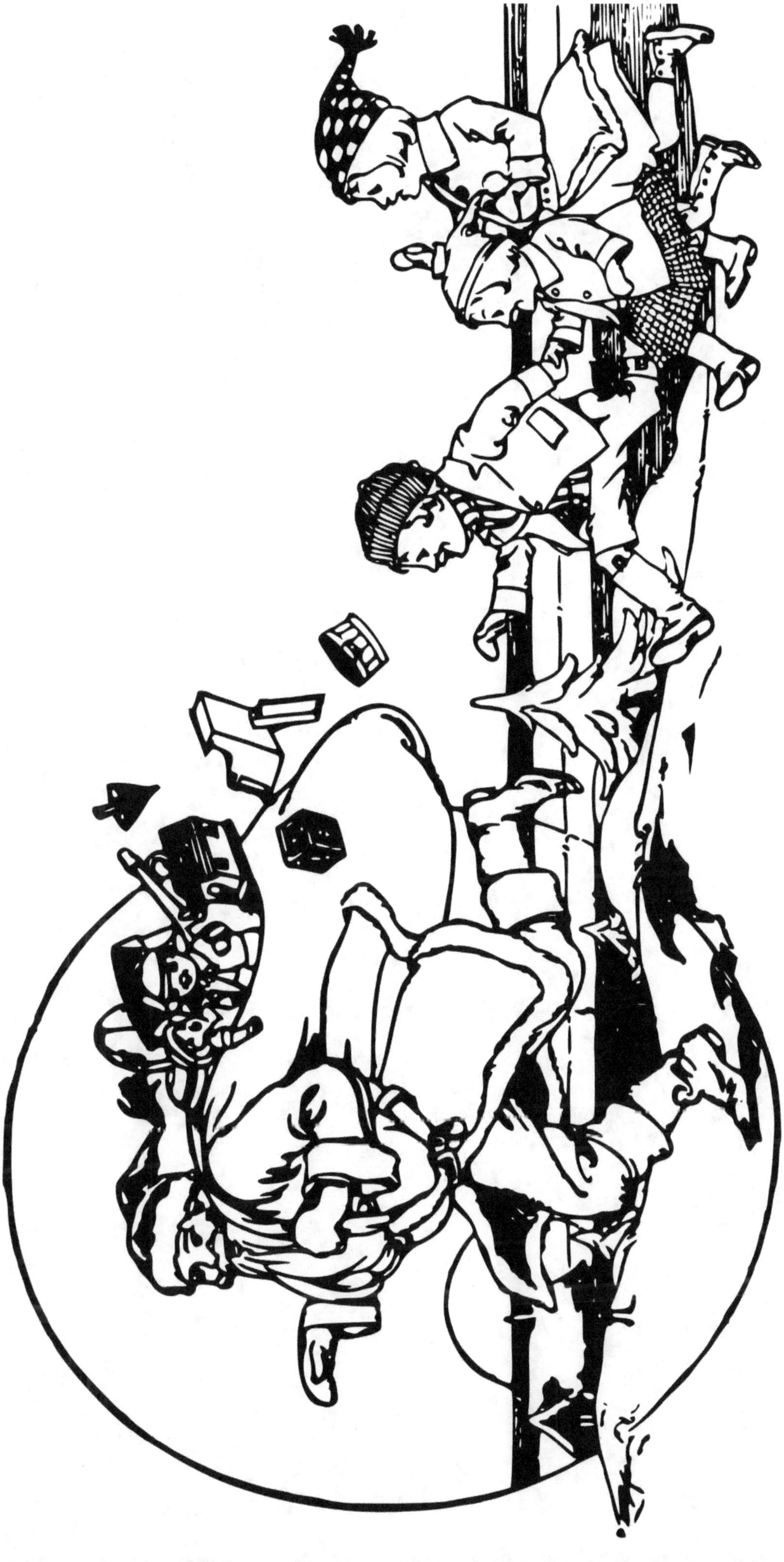

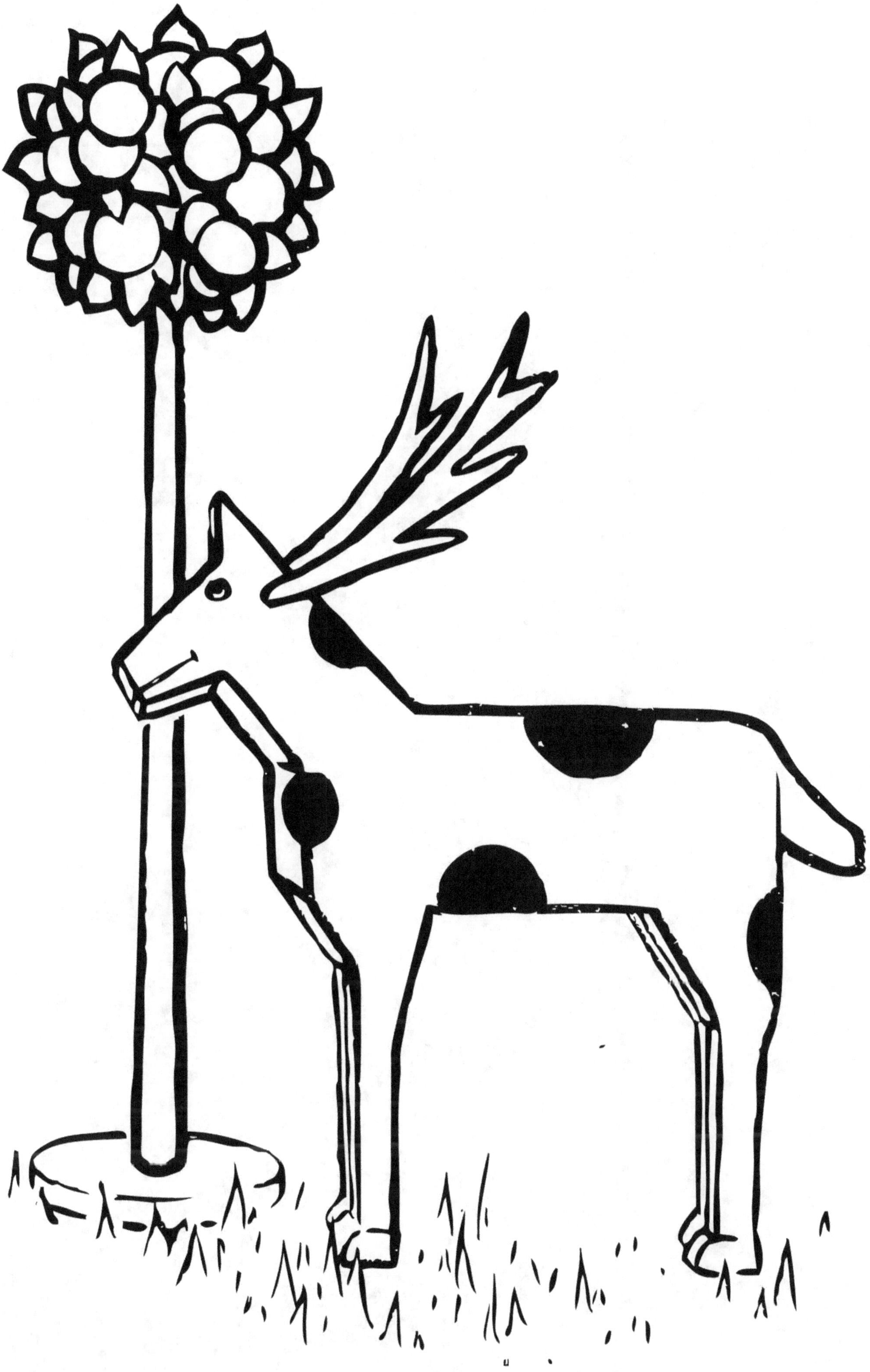

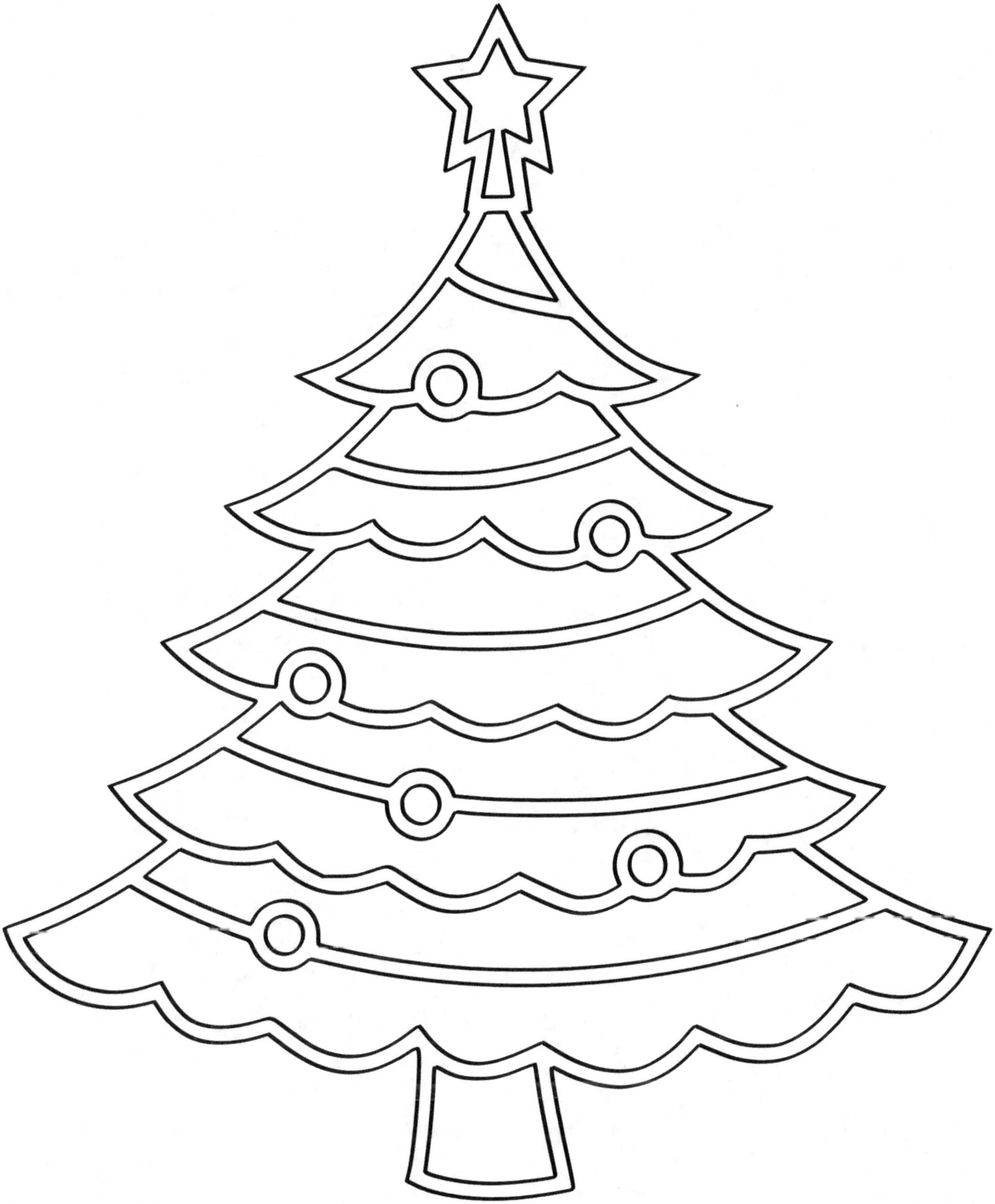

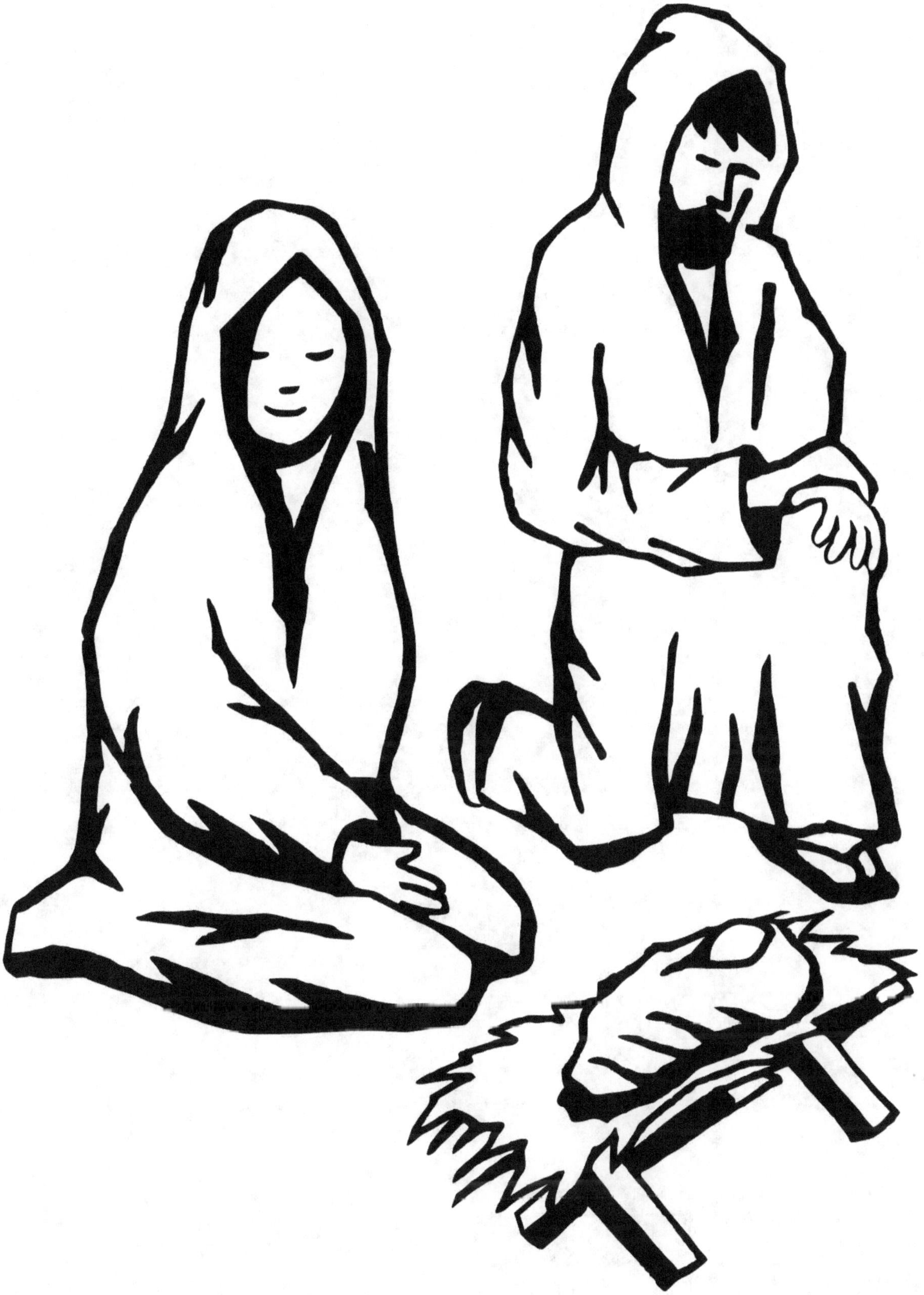

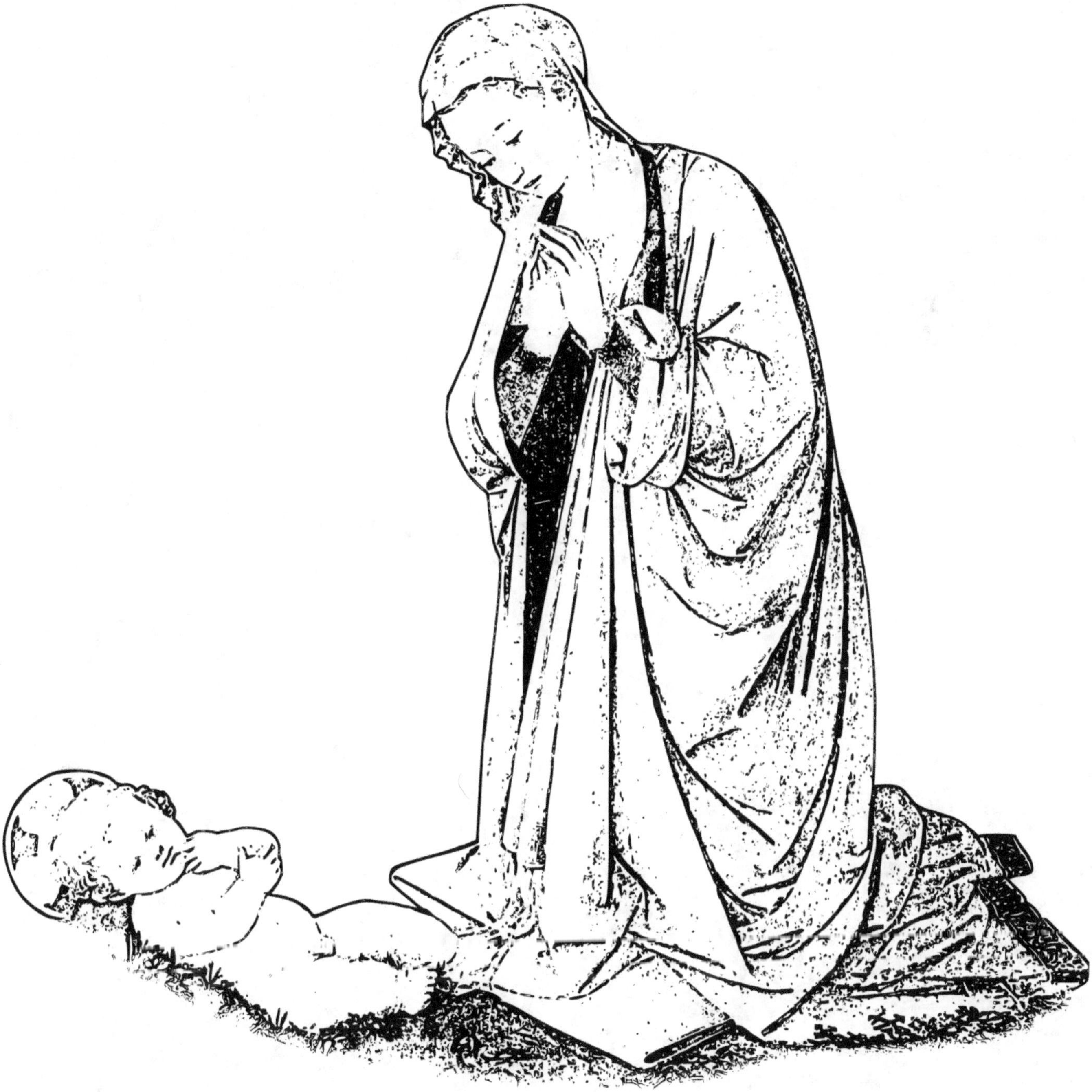

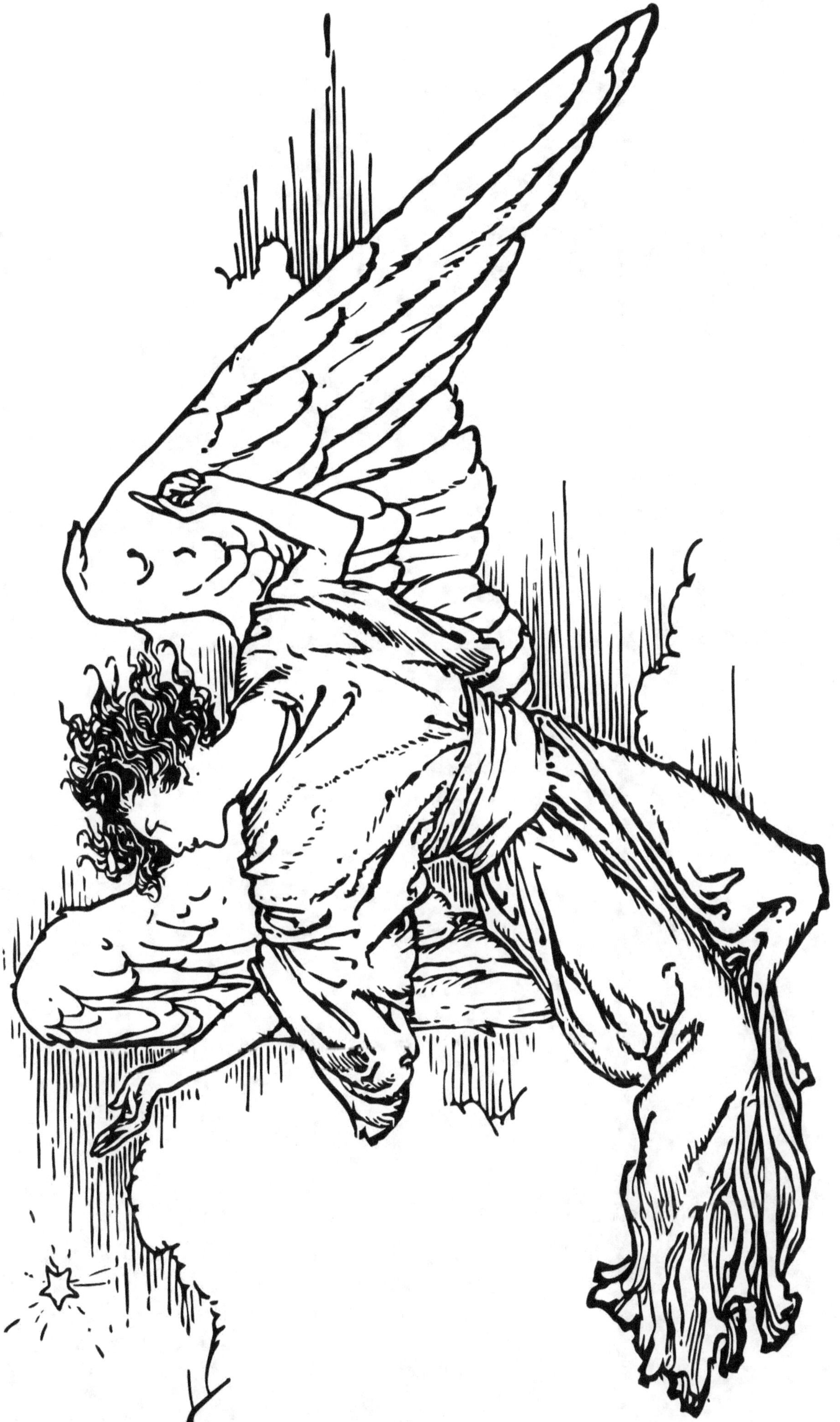

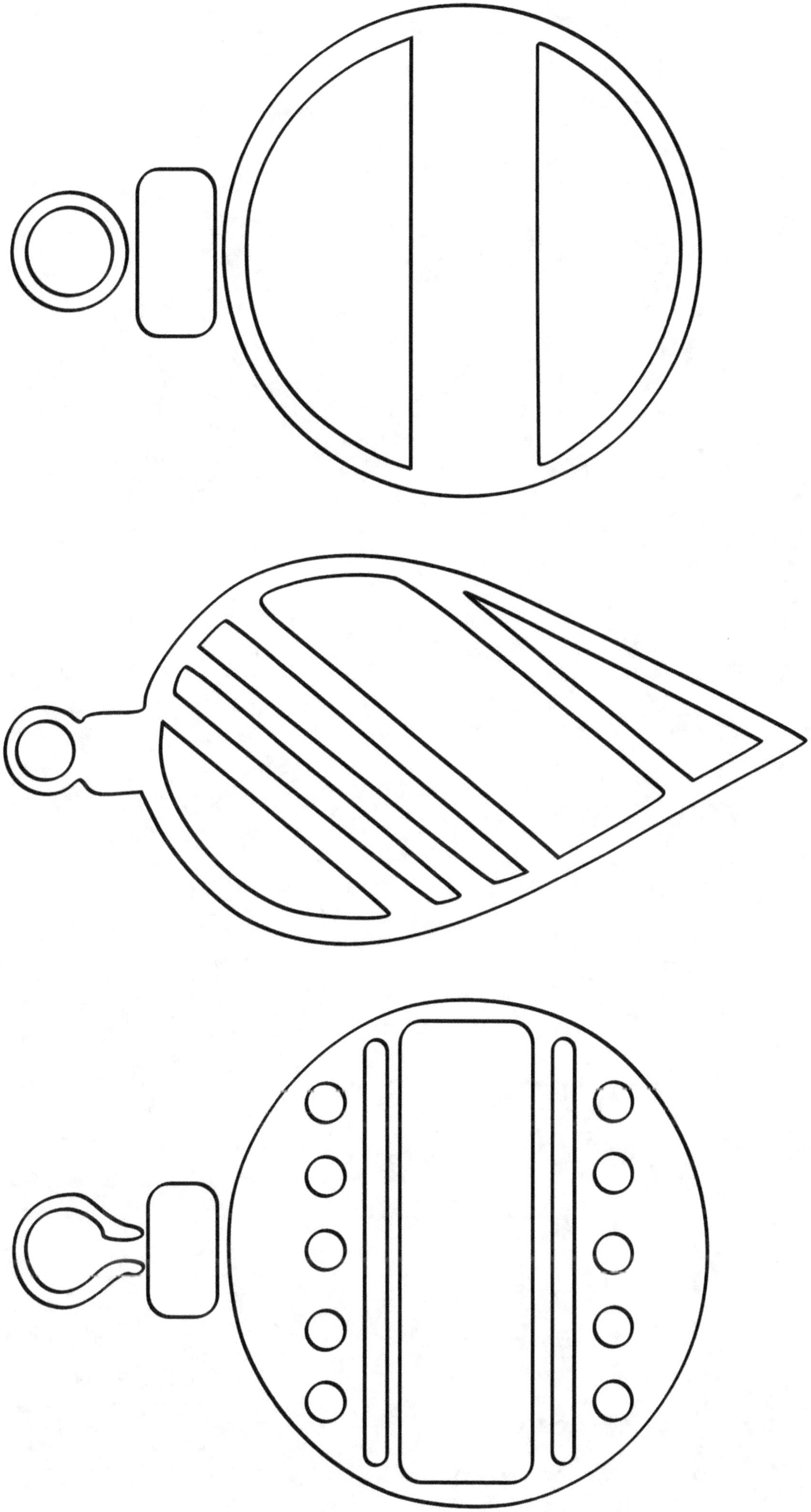

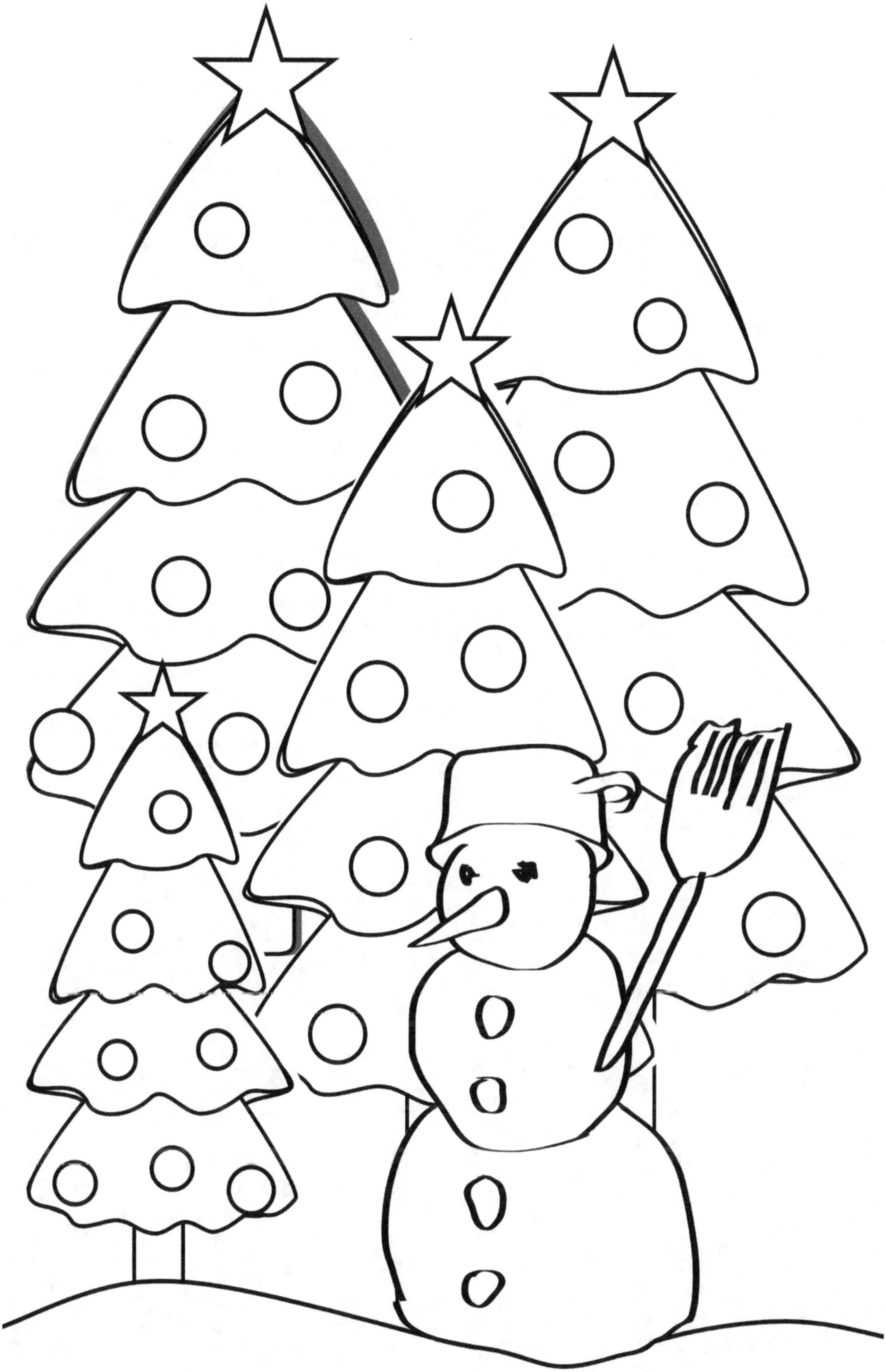

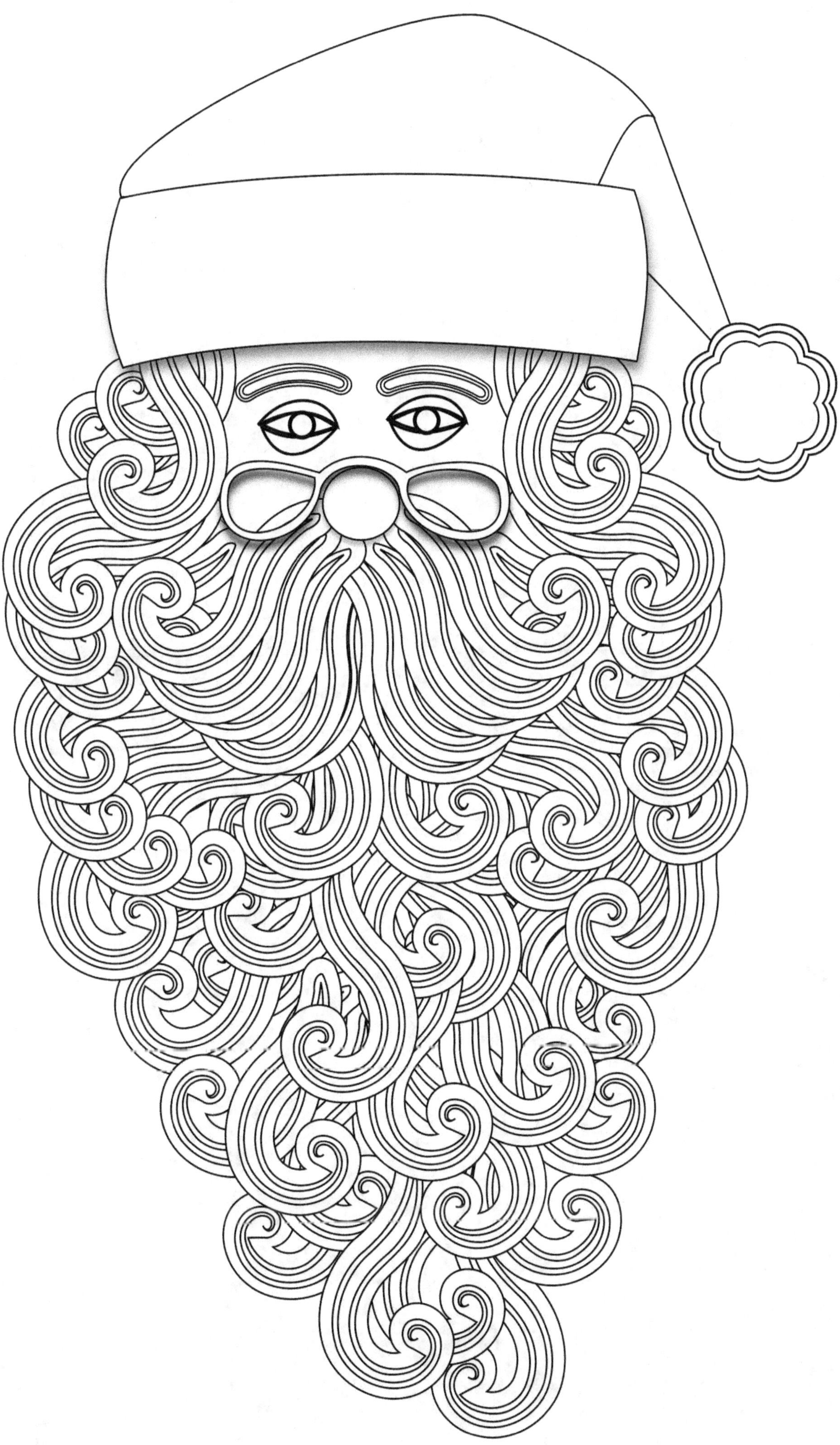

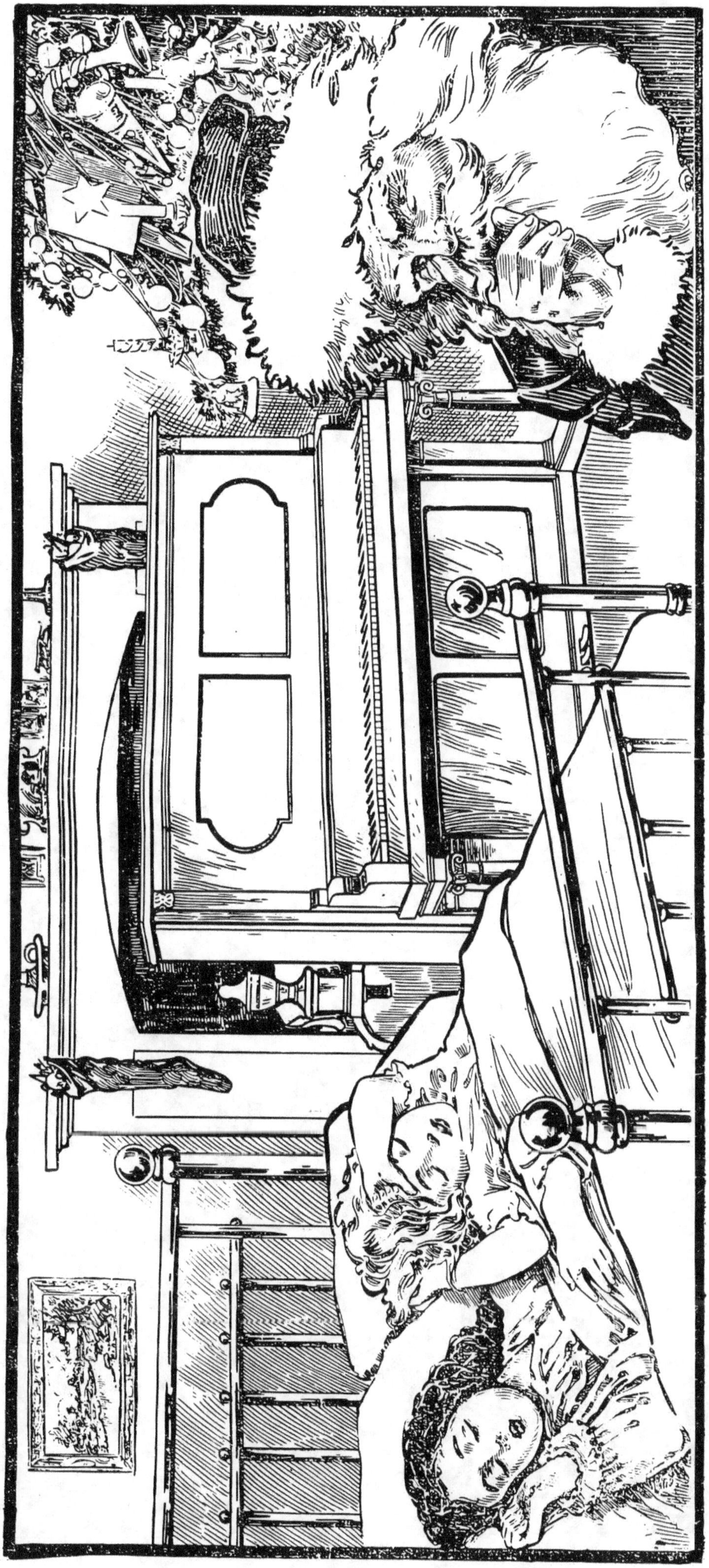

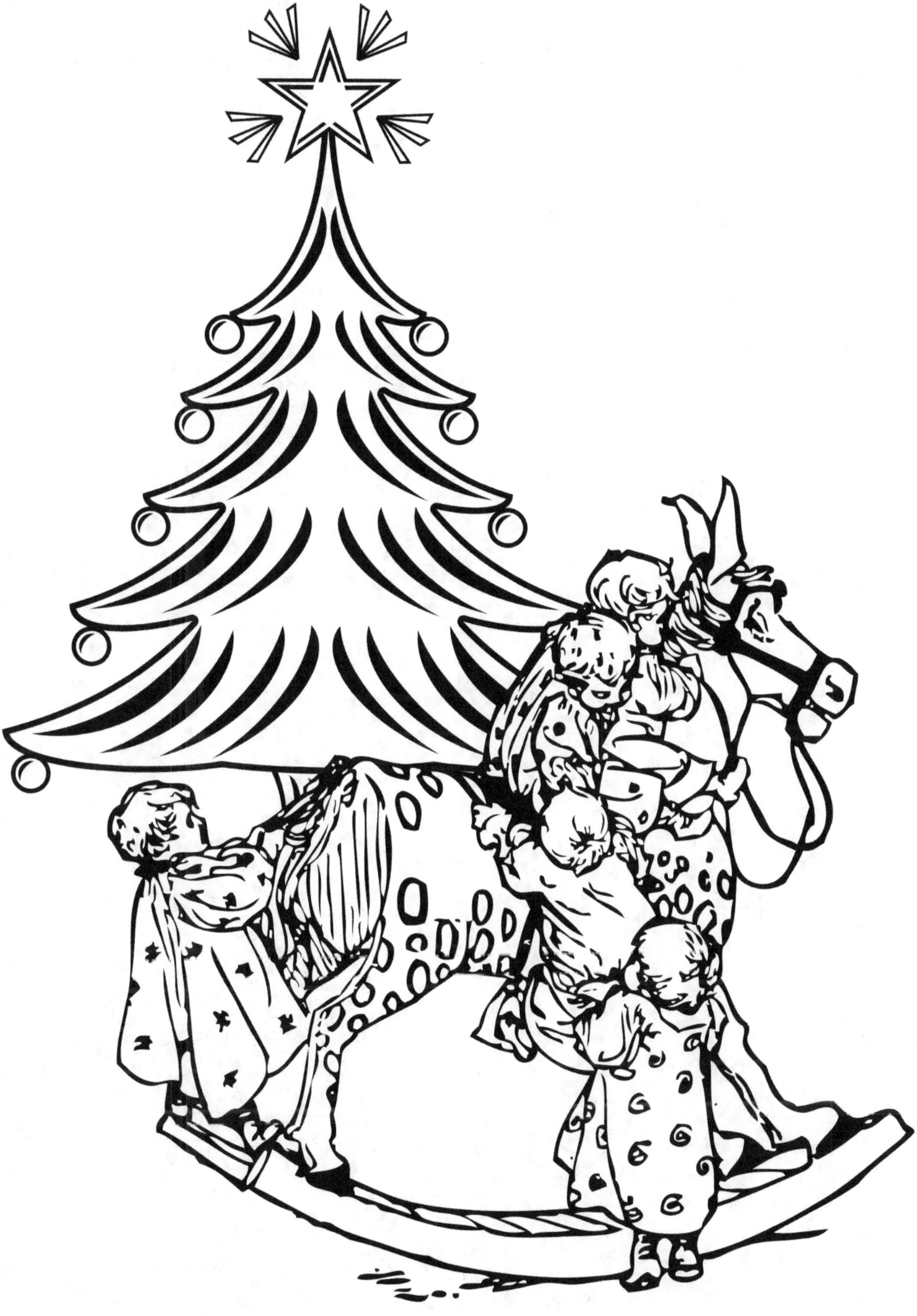

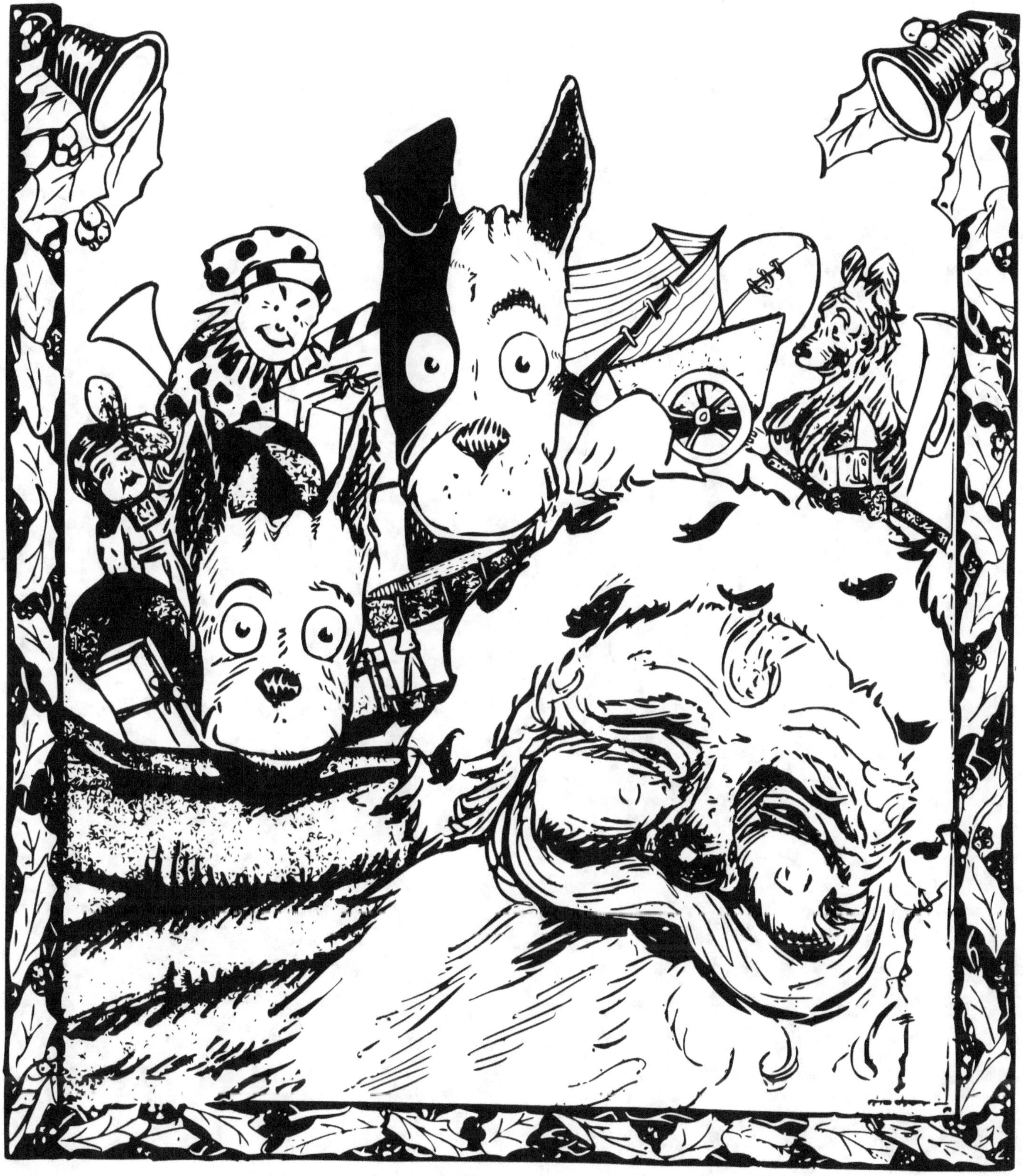

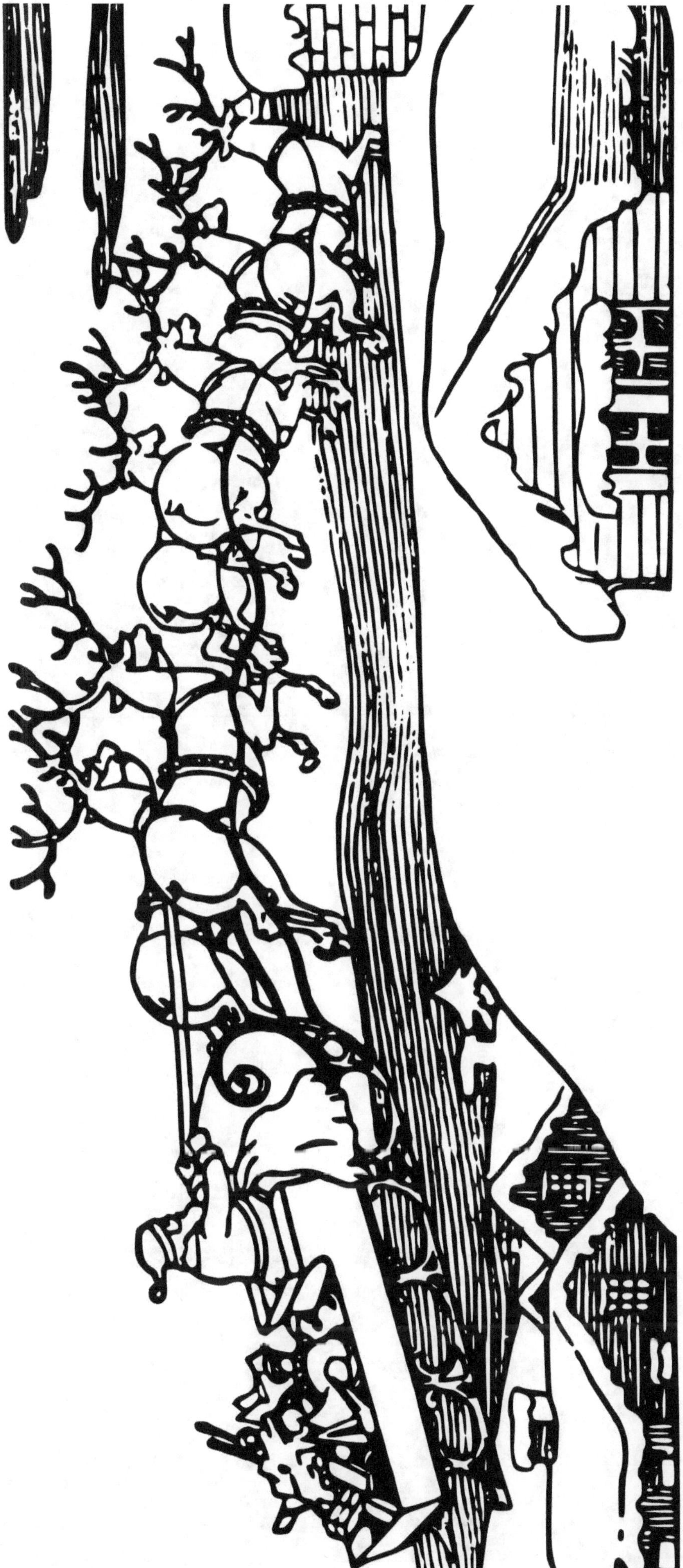

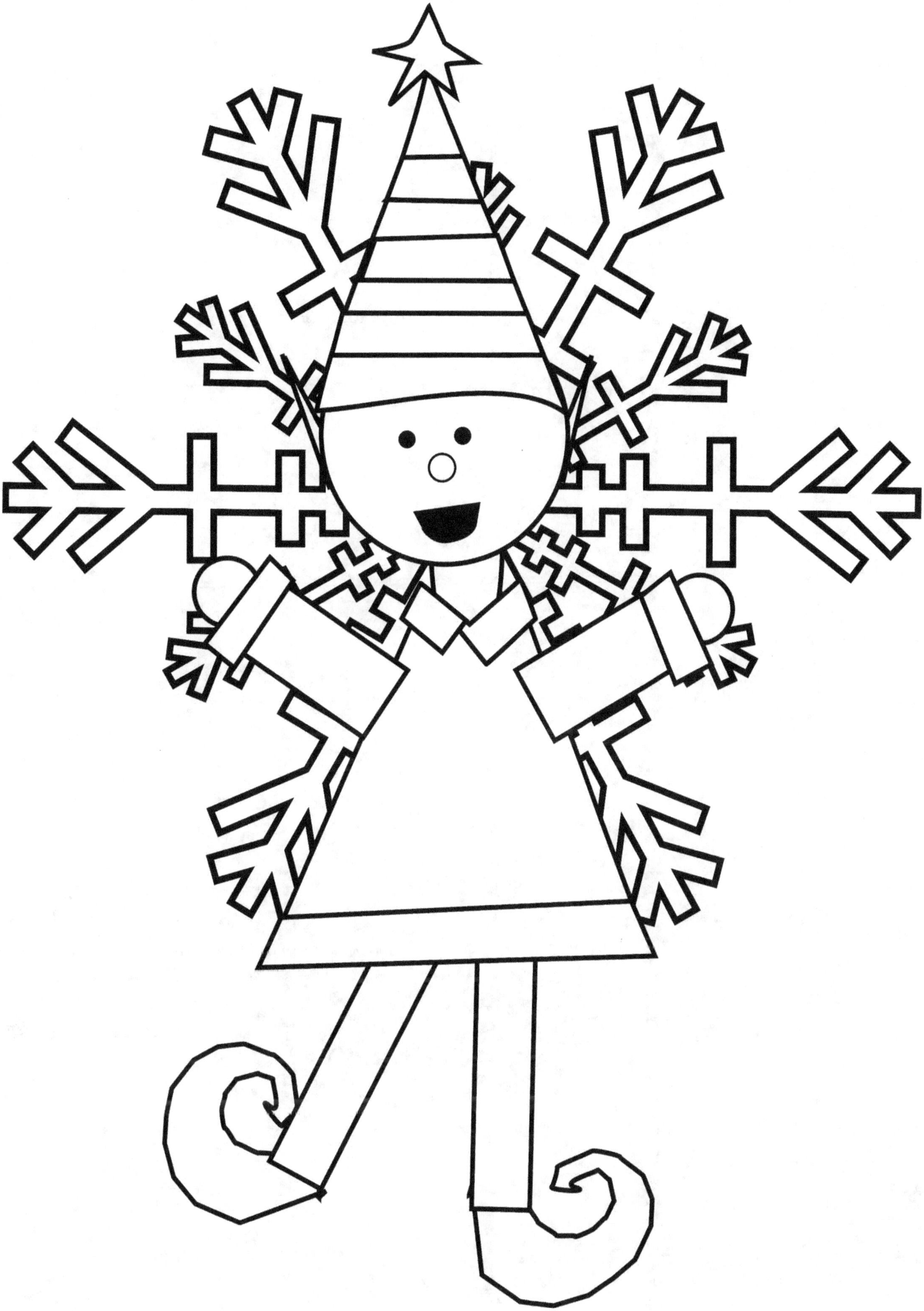

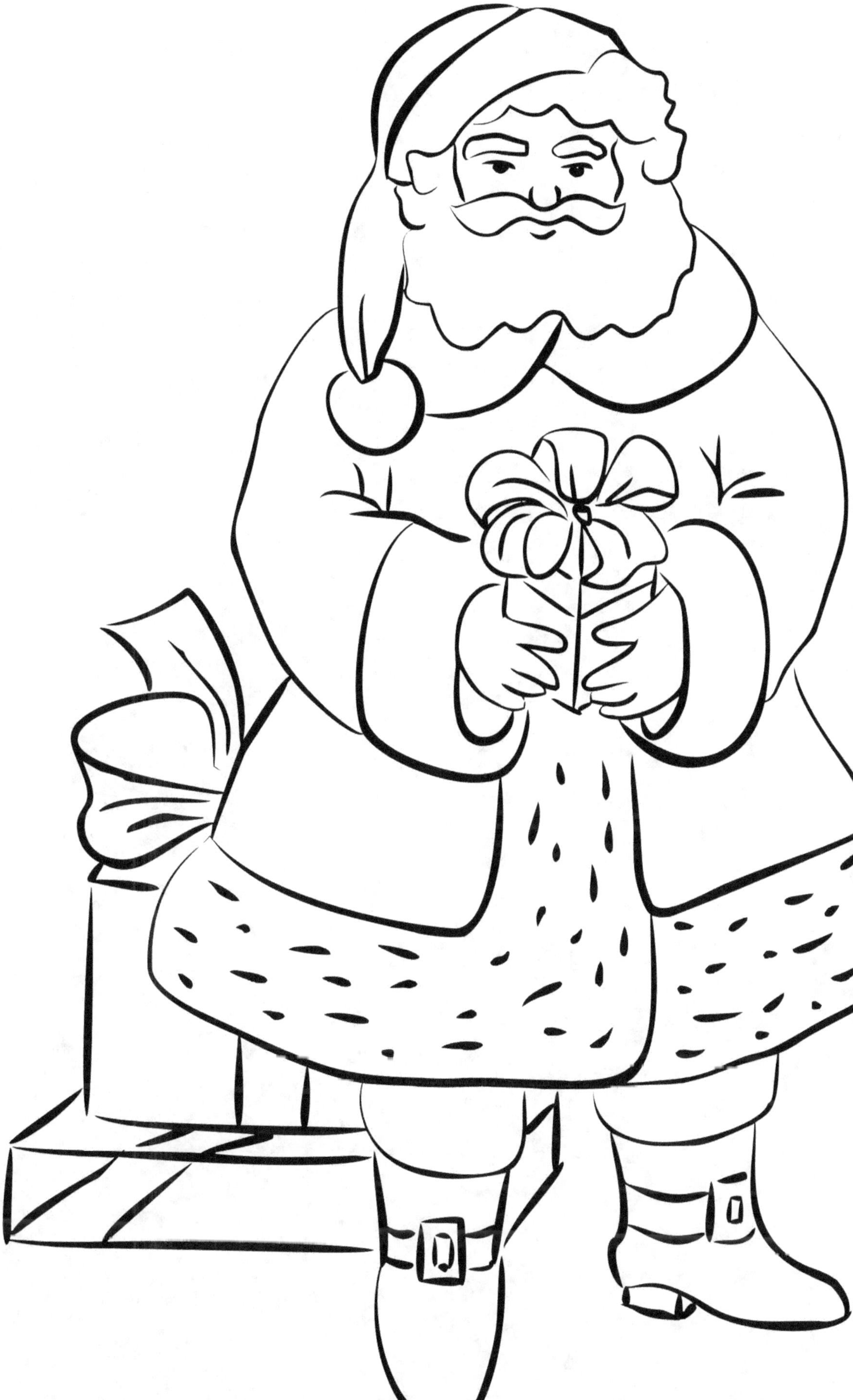

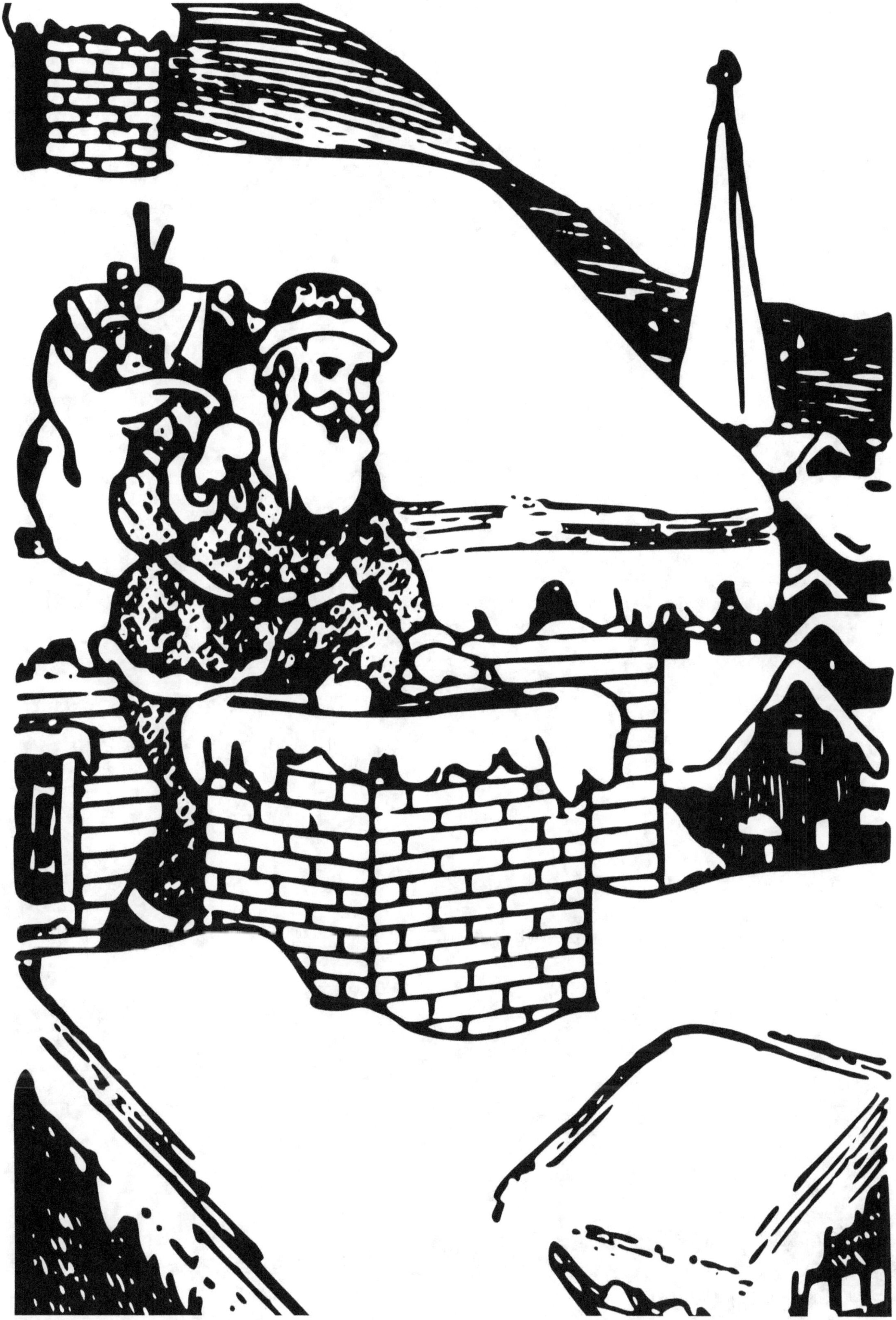

www.ingramcontent.com/pod-product-compliance
Lightning Source LLC
Chambersburg PA
CBHW081733220526
45468CB00008B/2077
* 9 7 8 1 9 8 1 5 2 0 6 4 0 *